ANCIENT EGYPT

GERALDINE HARRIS

THIRD EDITION

CHELSEA HOUSE
PUBLISHERS

An imprint of Infobase Publishing

Cultural Atlas for Young People
ANCIENT EGYPT
Third Edition

Copyright © 2007 The Brown Reference Group plc

Chelsea House
An imprint of Infobase Publishing
132 West 31st Street
New York, NY 10001

Library of Congress Cataloging-in-Publication Data available upon request.

ISBN: 0-8160-6823-2

ISBN 13 digit: 978-0-8160-6823-4

Set ISBN: 978-0-8160-7218-7

Chelsea House books are available at special discounts when purchased in bulk quantities for businesses, associations, institutions, or sales promotions. Please call our Special Sales Department in New York at (212) 967-8800 or (800) 322-8755.

You can find Chelsea House on the World Wide Web at:
http://www.chelseahouse.com

The Brown Reference Group
(incorporating Andromeda Oxford Limited)
8 Chapel Place, Rivington Street
London EC2A 3DQ
www.brownreference.com

For The Brown Reference Group plc:
Editorial Director: Lindsey Lowe
Project Editor: Graham Bateman
Editor: Virginia Carter
Design: Steve McCurdy
Senior Managing Editor: Tim Cooke

Printed in Singapore

10 9 8 7 6 5 4 3 2 1

Artwork and Picture Credits
All maps drawn by Lovell Johns, Oxford.

Key: t = top, b = bottom, c = center, l = left, r = right

Title page Rosalind Hall. 5 John Hillelson Agency. 6–7 Malcolm Smythe. 8–9 MH. 10 A.A.M. van der Heyden. 12t ME. 12b Hirmer Verlag, Munich. 15, 16 KM. 17l ME (Phaidon Press). 17tr R. Giveon, Mishmar Ha'emek. 17br University College, London. 18l Ägyptisches Museum, W. Berlin (Hirmer Verlag, Munich). 18r Museo Gregoriano Egizo, Vatican (Phaidon Press). 20t GI (Elsevier). 20b Coral Mula. 21t Rosalind Hall, London. 21b Coral Mula. 22tl Ash. 22tc Ash (Elsevier). 22tr Met. 23tl Nina M. Davies, Ancient Egyptian Paintings. 23tr MH. 23b Coral Mula. 24–25 KM. 25bl MH. 25r Ash (Elsevier). 26c GI (Elsevier). 26bl BM (MH). 26br Ash. (Elsevier). 27 CF. 28l,c Ash. (Elsevier). 28r Ash. 29 Ash. (Elsevier). 30t EM (RW). 30bl A.A.M. van der Heyden, Amsterdam. 30br EM (RW). 31 CF. 32t EM (Hirmer Verlag, Munich). 32bl Brooklyn Museum, New York. 32br EM (RW). 34t Museo Civico, Bologna (Alinari, Florence). 34bl D. Johannes, Cairo. 34br EM (RW). 36t A.A.M. van der Heyden. 36b KM. 38t Coral Mula. 38b, 39 BM. 40–41 KM. 42t EM (RW). 42b Fitzwilliam Museum, Cambridge. 43 Museum of Fine Arts, Boston. 44t University Museum, University of Pennsylvania. 44bl BM (MH). 44br EM. 46t BM. 46bl A.P. Zivie, Paris. 46bc EM (Drawing: JF). 46br BM. 48l BM (M H). 48t Akhmim-Czech Institute of Egyptology, Prague. 48r Milan Zemina, Archives of the Czech Institute of Egyptology, Charles University, Prague. 49t EM (RW). 49b The Mastaba of Mereruka, Chicago. 50–51 Robert Harding Picture Library. 52–53 D. Barnard, London. 54 GI. 56 RW. 56–57 KM. 57br CF. 58 RW. 60l A.A.M. van der Heyden, Amsterdam. 60r A.-P. Zivie, Paris. 61 A.A.M. van der Heyden, Amsterdam. 61r Institute of Archaeology, University of London (RAF). 62 John Hillelson Agency, London. 63 A.A.M. van der Heyden, Amsterdam. 64t Rosalind Hall, London. 64c MH. 64b Carmen Redondo/CORBIS. 65t A.A.M. van der Heyden, Amsterdam. 65b Roger Wood/CORBIS. 66t WF. 66b MH. 67t A.-P. Zivie, Paris. 67b Rosalind Hall, London. 68 GI. 68–69 KM. 69 John Hillelson Agency, London. 70 A.M. Calverley, The Temple of King Sethos of Abydos, London & Chicago. 71 A.-P. Zivie, Paris. 72 A.A.M. van der Heyden, Amsterdam. 73l Werner Forman Archive/Egyptian Museum, Cairo. 73r J. Baines, Oxford. 73b Werner Forman Archive. 74t Met. 74b D. Johannes, Cairo. 76l Museum of Fine Arts, Boston. 76r Rosalind Hall, London. 77t A.A.M. van der Heyden, Amsterdam. 77c D. Barnard, London. 77b Ash (Elsevier). 78, 79 CF. 80t Ash (Elsevier). 80b RW. 82t EM (Drawing: JF). 82bl Rosalind Hall, London. 82br EM (Hirmer Verlag, Munich). 83l EM (RW). 83cr Rosalind Hall, London. 83br Egypt Exploration Society, London. 84t Staatliche Museum, E. Berlin. 84b D. Johannes, Cairo. 85t J. Baines, Oxford. 85b A.A.M. van der Heyden. 86–87 CF. 88 Museo Civico, Bologna (Fotofast, Bologna). 90l Ash (Elsevier). 90r Stéphane Compoint. 91l Dean Conger/CORBIS. 91r Romer-Pelizaeus-Museum, Hildesheim.

List of Abbreviations
Ash = Ashmolean Museum, Oxford; BM British Museum, London; CF = Chris Forsey; EM = Egyptian Museum, Cairo; GI = Griffith Institute, Ashmolean Museum, Oxford; KM = Kevin Maddison; ME = Museo Egizio, Turin; Met = Metropolitan Museum of Art, New York; MH = Michael Holford, Loughton; RW = Roger Wood, London; WF = Werner Forman, London.

Contents

Introduction

THIS BOOK IS ABOUT ANCIENT EGYPT, ONE OF THE GREAT civilizations of the past. The ancient Greeks saw Egypt as the source of all wisdom. Roman emperors traveled to Egypt to marvel at monuments such as the pyramids. Egyptian statues and obelisks were sent to decorate Rome. The worship of Egyptian gods and goddesses such as Isis and Osiris spread through the Roman Empire as far as Britain.

The modern fascination with Egypt began in the late 18th century. Since then, a huge number of ancient towns, temples, and tombs have been excavated. No country in the world has so many impressive ancient remains as Egypt does. In the Nile Valley the past seems very close. The people who lived there thousands of years ago have left us a wonderful legacy of art and architecture and literature.

Ancient Egypt is divided into two main sections. The first, **The History of the Pharaohs**, tells the story of Egypt from the union of the country in about 3100 B.C.E. to the coming of the Romans almost 3,000 years later. Archaeologists break up the great span of Egyptian history into a series of periods and "kingdoms." You can see how this works by looking at the Timelines on pages 6 and 7.

The Predynastic Period was the era before Egypt was united under a single ruler. From the Early Dynastic Period, Egypt was ruled by dynasties of kings. A dynasty was a sequence of rulers, usually related by blood or marriage. The eras known as kingdoms were times when Egypt was strong and united. The "intermediate periods," which come between or after kingdoms, were times when the country was weak and divided. The last dynasties of native Egyptian kings ruled during the Late Period, so called because it comes at the end of Egypt's history as an independent nation. In the Greco-Roman Period, Egypt was first under Greek and then under Roman rule.

On each history double-page spread you will find a list of the dynasties that reigned during that period or kingdom. The names and dates of the most important rulers in each dynasty are also given. The exact spelling and pronunciation of most ancient Egyptian names is uncertain because vowels were not written in full. Ideas about how the names should be written out in English have changed as our knowledge of ancient languages has grown. The name that used to be spelled Tutankhamen is now usually written as Tutankhamun or Tutankhamon. It means "Living Image of the god Amon."

The maps in the first part of the book are linked to topics in the text. They show you which places were important in each period or kingdom or sites where objects of a particular date have been found.

The second part of this book, **A Journey Down the Nile**, takes you the length of Egypt. The journey starts in Lower Nubia, a country to the south of Egypt, and ends at the Mediterranean coast. There is a map for each region. These are maps of modern Egypt but they mark all the important ancient sites and structures that survive. For most sites a modern Arabic name and at least one ancient name are given. Some of these ancient names are Egyptian. Others date to the time when the Greeks ruled Egypt. Beside the site names are symbols to show you what kind of ancient remains have been found there.

The Glossary on pages 92–93 explains the Egyptian, Greek, and archaeological terms used in this book. If you want to look up a particular place, the Gazetteer on page 94 will tell you how to locate it.

Abbreviations used in this book
B.C.E. = Before Common Era (also known as B.C.).
C.E. = Common Era (also known as A.D.). c. = *circa* (about).
in = inch; ft = foot; yd = yard; mi = mile.
cm = centimeter; m = meter; km = kilometer.

▶ The feet of a pharaoh. Detail of an 18th-Dynasty granite statue in Luxor temple with a later cartouche.

Timelines

	4500 B.C.E.	3500 B.C.E.	3000 B.C.E.	2500 B.C.E.
EGYPTIAN HISTORY	**Predynastic** Badarian/Tasian culture, Nile valley c.4500–4000. Merimda cultures, Delta c.4800–4100. Faiyum culture c.5400–4400.	**Predynastic** Naqada I, Nile valley c.4000–3500. Naqada II–III, Nile valley c.3500–3100. Invention of writing.	**Foundation of Egyptian state c.3100.** Trade with Mesopotamia. **Early Dynastic Period c.2920–2575.** 1st–3rd Dynasties. First mining expeditions to Sinai.	**Old Kingdom c.2575–2134.** 4th–6th Dynasties. Raids on Libya, Palestine, and Lower Nubia. Trade with Upper Nubia. **First Intermediate Period c.2134–2040** 7th–11th Dynasties. Rival dynasties and civil wars.
	Hunters from stone palette, c.3000 B.C.E.		*Tomb stela of King Wadj from Abydos, c.2980 B.C.E.*	*Statue of King Khephren from Giza, c.2495 B.C.E.*

Hunters from stone palette, c.3000 B.C.E.

Tomb stela of King Wadj from Abydos, c.2980 B.C.E.

Statue of King Khephren from Giza, c.2495 B.C.E.

	4500 B.C.E.	3500 B.C.E.	3000 B.C.E.	2500 B.C.E.
ARCHITECTURE AND TOMBS	Reed huts. Graves under hut floors at Merimda Beni Salama.	Reed shrines. First buildings in mud-brick. Walled town and brick-lined tombs at Hierakonpolis.	Mud-brick "funerary palaces" at Abydos. Mud-brick *mastaba* tombs at Saqqara. First stone buildings.	Massive stone pyramids and stone *mastaba* tombs at Giza, Saqqara, and Abusir. Stone sun temples and obelisks at Abu Ghurab and Abusir.

Painted terra-cotta figurine of a dancer, c.4000 B.C.E.

Painting of geese from a tomb at Maidum, c.2560 B.C.E.

Step pyramids at Saqqara.

Step Pyramid of King Djoser at Saqqara, c.2560 B.C.E.

	4500 B.C.E.	3500 B.C.E.	3000 B.C.E.	2500 B.C.E.
ART AND CRAFTS	Fine pottery vessels, clay figurines, objects carved from ivory.	Painted pottery, stone palettes and vessels, terra-cotta and ivory figurines. First wall paintings and stone statuettes.	Large stone statues. First reliefs in wood and stone. First stone stelae. Gold jewelry. Faience figurines.	Painted tomb reliefs of daily life. Royal statues in hard stones or in copper. Private statues in stone or wood. Furniture in wood and decorated sheet gold.

Middle Kingdom c.2040–1640.
11th–13th Dynasties.
Reunion of Egypt under Theban dynasty.
Trade with Syria and Palestine.
Occupation of Lower Nubia.

Second Intermediate Period c.1640–1532.
14th–17th Dynasties.
Occupation of Delta by Hyksos from Syria/Palestine.
Kerma culture occupies Lower Nubia.
War between the Hyksos and Theban kings.

Statue of King Senwosret III from Deir el-Bahri, c.1850 B.C.E.

Early New Kingdom 1550–1307.
17th–18th Dynasties.

Egypt reunited under Theban dynasty.

Conquest of Lower and Upper Nubia.

Rise of Egyptian empire in Syria and Palestine.

Gold mask from the mummy of King Tutankhamon, c.1325 B.C.E.

Late New Kingdom c.1307–1196.
19th–20th Dynasties. Wars against the Hittites in Syria.

Depopulation of Lower Nubia.

Wars against the Sea Peoples.

Gradual loss of Near Eastern empire.

Colossal statue at the Great Temple of Abu Simbel, c.1270 B.C.E.

Third Intermediate Period c.1070–712.
21st–25th Dynasties.
Egypt divided.
Kings ruling Delta and High Priests ruling Thebes.
Rise of Nubian Kingdom of Napata.
Civil wars among petty rulers.

Late Period 712–332.
25th–30th Dynasties
Egypt reunited by Nubian kings.
Conquest of Egypt by the Assyrians and by the Persians.
Periods of native rule between conquests.

Kneeling Egyptian from statue base of a Persian king, c.500 B.C.E.

Greco-Roman Period 332 B.C.E.–395 C.E.
Greek rule 332–30 B.C.E.
Egypt ruled by Ptolemies.
Many Greek immigrants. Some Egyptian rebellions.
Roman rule 30 B.C.E.–395 C.E.
Egypt becomes part of the Roman Empire.
Most of Nubia ruled by Kings of Meroe.

Head of a priest in green schist, c.75 B.C.E.

Stone mortuary temple of Mentuhotep III at Deir el-Bahri.

Mud-brick pyramids in Middle Egypt and at Dahshur.

Rock-cut tombs in Middle Egypt.

Forts in Nubia.

Wooden figurine of a servant from a Theban tomb, c.2020 B.C.E.

Terraced temple of Hatshepsut at Deir el-Bahri.

Rock-cut royal tombs in the Valley of the Kings.

Temples of Amon at Karnak and Luxor.

Palaces and Aten temples at el-Amarna.

Relief from a vizier's tomb at Thebes, c.1360 B.C.E.

Mortuary temples of Ramesses II (The Ramesseum) and Ramesses III (Medinet Habu) at Thebes.

Great Hypostyle Hall at Karnak, Ramesses II.

Great Temple of Abu Simbel and other rock-cut and freestanding temples in Nubia.

Relief of a blind harpist from a Saqqara tomb, c.1300 B.C.E.

Temple of Amon at Tanis with underground royal tombs.

Large tombs with mud-brick pylons at Thebes.

Shaft tombs at Saqqara.

Granite temple of Isis at Behbeit el-Hagar.

Inlaid bronze figure of a high priestess, c.850 B.C.E.

Great Egyptian-style temples at Philae, Kom Ombo, Edfu, Esna, and Dendara.

Greco-Egyptian style "funerary houses" at Tuna el-Gebel.

Underground galleries of tombs at Alexandria.

Facade of the temple of Hathor at Dendara, c.34 C.E.

Royal portrait sculpture.

Tomb paintings of daily life.

Painted wooden models of daily life.

Fine jewelry in gold and semiprecious stones.

Temple reliefs with royal and religious scenes.

Monumental sculpture.

Tomb paintings and painted reliefs of daily life.

Decorated pottery and faience vessels.

Colossal stone statues.

Temple reliefs with battle and hunting scenes.

Illustrated "Books of the Dead."

Tomb paintings of religious scenes.

Faience bowls and chalices.

Bronze figurines.

Private sculpture in hard stones.

Decorated cartonnage coffins and stone sarcophagi.

Portrait sculpture in hard stones.

Temple reliefs of religious scenes.

Faience and terra-cotta figurines.

Painted "mummy portraits."

Part One

The History
of the Pharaohs

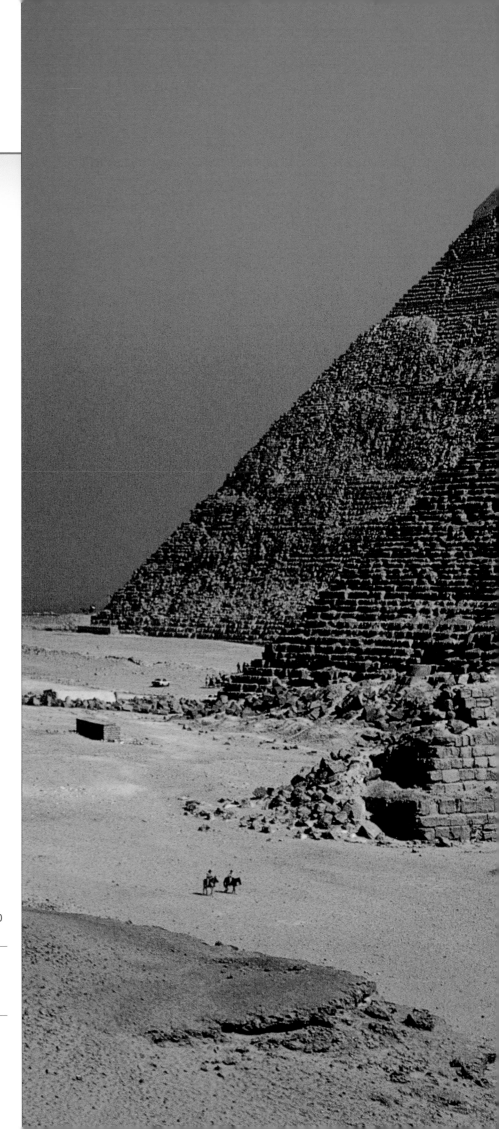

▲ Detail from the golden throne found in Tutankhamon's tomb by the English Egyptologist Howard Carter in 1922.

▶ The 4,500-year-old pyramids at Giza, to the southwest of Cairo, the present-day capital of Egypt. The two largest are more than 330 ft (100 m) high.

Egypt, Gift of the Nile

ABOUT 12,000 YEARS AGO MOST OF NORTH Africa was covered by savanna—grasslands inhabited by large populations of animals. Gradually the climate became drier, and slowly the savanna turned to desert. The longest river in the world—the Nile River—flowed through this desert, with rich vegetation along its valley.

The Nile valley is a long, narrow corridor that is never more than l2 miles (19 km) and sometimes as little as 1 mile (1.6 km) wide. Before joining the Mediterranean, the river splits into many branches. This Delta area is some 125 miles (200 km) across.

The Black Land and the Red Land

The ancient Egyptians referred to their country as the Black Land. Black was the color of the rich soil in the Nile valley. The valley had once been a swamp, but as the climate changed only the Delta retained large areas of marshland.

Every year summer rains in Africa caused the waters of the Nile to rise along its length, flooding the low-lying fields in Egypt for about two months. The area covered in water was known as the floodplain and the event was called the inundation. When the waters went down they left a layer of fertile mud that was ideal for growing crops in. The level of the inundation was important. A low ("bad")

Nile meant that only part of the floodplain would be covered and not enough crops could be grown to feed everyone. A very high Nile (also called bad) might flood villages and towns.

To the east and west of the Nile valley lie the deserts, which the Egyptians called the Red Land. The valley dwellers thought of the Red Land as a dangerous and sinister place. The few oases in the Western Desert were sometimes used as prison camps. The mountainous Eastern Desert was divided by dry riverbeds called wadis, which occasionally filled after heavy rains. These wadis became trade routes across the desert to the coast of the Red Sea.

To the south of Egypt the Nile becomes difficult to sail because of the rapids known as the Cataracts. To the north of the country, Egypt was protected by the marshes of the delta. These natural barriers made Egypt a difficult country to invade. Its isolation from the rest of the ancient world helps to explain the unique culture of Egypt.

▼ An ancient scene in modern Egypt at Abusir near Cairo. Palms are growing in the arable land. The pyramids are nearly 4,500 years old.

▶ The geography of Egypt today. The Nile is fed by the Blue and the White Nile. Its ultimate source is Lake Victoria, located in the south of Uganda.

Feet
6,500
1,650
650
0
Below sea level

△▽8660 Spot height (feet)
—·—·— International boundary
■ Capital city
● Other settlement
○ Oasis
Marsh
--------- Wadi (dry river bed)

Scale 1:15 000 000

0   400 km

0   300 miles

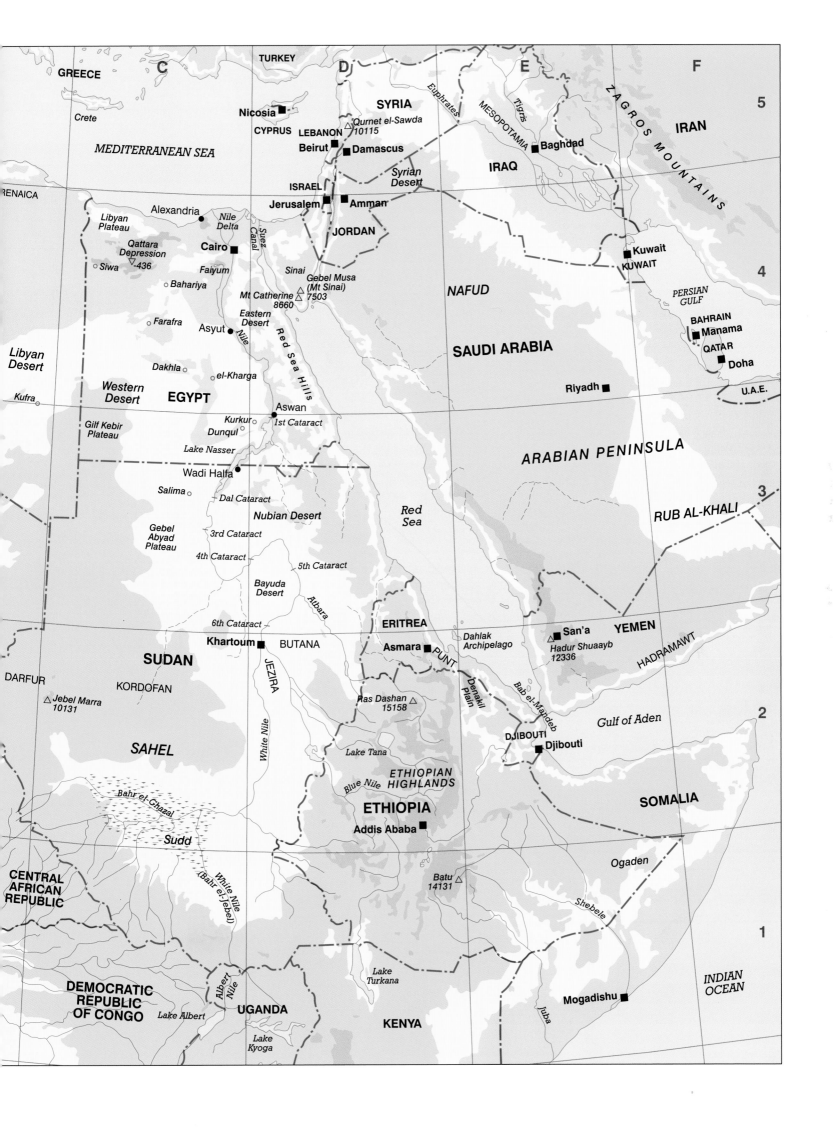

The Land of Gold

THE DESERT HILLS ON THE EDGE OF THE Nile provided limestone, sandstone, and granite for building temples and tombs. Rarer stones such as diorite, alabaster, and basalt were mainly used for vases and statues.

The Egyptian deserts also contained various semiprecious stones and precious metals—particularly gold. One foreign king wrote to the pharaoh that it was well known that in Egypt gold was as common as dust.

The Nile—Egypt's first resource

The most precious resource in ancient Egypt was water. The annual inundation made it possible to grow cereal crops such as corn and barley. Another major crop grown was flax. This was spun into linen. The best ancient Egyptian linen is so fine that you can see through it.

Irrigation channels were dug to carry water far from the Nile to people's gardens and orchards. Vegetables such as lettuce, onions, peas, and lentils were raised, and fruits such as pomegranates and figs were grown.

Wet clay from the riverbank was shaped into bricks that were left to dry in the sun. All Egyptian houses were built using this mud-brick.

▶ Pieces from the oldest known map, which dates to the 12th century B.C.E. The map shows stone quarries and gold mines in the Wadi Hammamat, a valley in the Eastern Desert. It was used by an expedition sent to bring back a colossal royal statue that was cut in the quarries. The Egyptian script mentions both natural and man-made landmarks.

▼ In this scene from a 19th-Dynasty tomb a couple are working in paradise—which is, of course, just like Egypt. In the top row they cut ears of corn. The middle row shows them harvesting flax and plowing a field. Below is a garden with date palms and ornamental plants.

Only in the Delta was there enough grass to feed large numbers of cattle, so most herds were kept there. The marshes were very rich in fish, bird, and plant life. The Egyptians caught fish with nets or spears and also hunted birds with boomerangs. Lotus flowers were gathered to make perfumes and reeds were cut to build boats or to weave into matting. The stems of papyrus plants were made into a kind of paper—one of Egypt's chief exports (see pages 22–23).

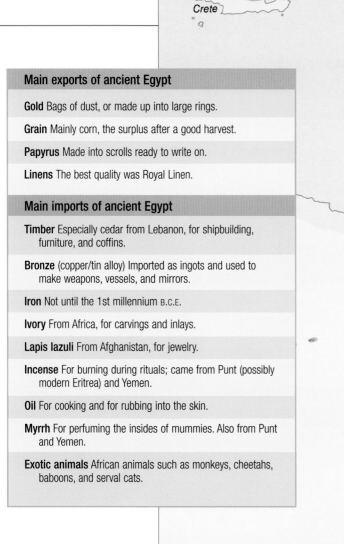

Main exports of ancient Egypt

Gold Bags of dust, or made up into large rings.

Grain Mainly corn, the surplus after a good harvest.

Papyrus Made into scrolls ready to write on.

Linens The best quality was Royal Linen.

Main imports of ancient Egypt

Timber Especially cedar from Lebanon, for shipbuilding, furniture, and coffins.

Bronze (copper/tin alloy) Imported as ingots and used to make weapons, vessels, and mirrors.

Iron Not until the 1st millennium B.C.E.

Ivory From Africa, for carvings and inlays.

Lapis lazuli From Afghanistan, for jewelry.

Incense For burning during rituals; came from Punt (possibly modern Eritrea) and Yemen.

Oil For cooking and for rubbing into the skin.

Myrrh For perfuming the insides of mummies. Also from Punt and Yemen.

Exotic animals African animals such as monkeys, cheetahs, baboons, and serval cats.

► Natural resources of Egypt. This map shows the very limited area of land that could be used for agriculture. The area of fertile land, particularly within the Delta, varied from season to season, year to year. Also marked are ancient mineral workings on the edges of the Nile valley and in the deserts. The turquoise mines of Sinai were highly prized by the Egyptians. The wadis (dry riverbeds) were used as trade routes. Other desert trade routes are shown on the map on page 33.

The Two Kingdoms

THE RULERS OF ANCIENT EGYPT WERE known as the Lords of the Two Lands—the kings of Upper and Lower Egypt. Upper Egypt was the narrow Nile valley. Lower Egypt was the north, particularly the Delta. The Two Lands were first united under one ruler in about 3100 B.C.E. The site of the capital of the union changed as families from different areas came to the throne. Several of these capital cities are located near the boundary of Upper and Lower Egypt, an area that is sometimes known as Middle Egypt.

Administrative centers

Until Greco-Roman times the population of ancient Egypt was probably never much more than 4 million people. Both Upper and Lower Egypt were divided into districts called nomes, and each one had its own administrative center. These centers would not have been large. Most Egyptians lived on farms or in small villages. Each village had a headman and each nome a governor, or nomarch.

The nomarchs ruled their districts on behalf of the kings but if the central government was weak they often tried to take power for themselves. Among the nomarchs' most important jobs were the upkeep of dykes and irrigation channels and the storing and distribution of grain to feed the local population during times of famine.

The first civil servants

In Egypt's capital a very large number of officials worked for the central government. The most important official was the vizier. He was in charge of justice and public works. At some periods there were two viziers, one for Upper and one for Lower Egypt. The vizier's office oversaw the collection of taxes. Until it came under Greek rule, Egypt had no coinage. All taxes therefore had to be paid with goods such as grain and cattle. A register of land ownership was kept and every two years all the cattle in Egypt were counted.

The officials who worked under the vizier had to be good at many different jobs. One official, called Weni, tells us in an inscription that during his career he was an inspector of pyramids, a judge, as well as a tax collector. Weni also led an army, supervised the digging of canals and the quarrying of stone for pyramids, and eventually became governor of the whole of southern Egypt. Successful officials like Weni were rewarded by being given luxury goods and country estates.

14

Upper Egypt

1	9	17
2	10	18
3	11	19
4	12	20
5	13	21
6	14	22
7	15	
8	16	

Lower Egypt

1	8	15
2	9	16
3	10	17
4	11	18
5	12	19
6	13	20
7	14	

▲ Each district, or nome, had a symbol. These symbols, or ensigns, were often derived from the form of a local god or goddess. In temple reliefs (carved scenes) the symbols are worn on the heads of figures that represent the nomes.

◄ The nomes of Upper Egypt. The boundaries of the 22 nomes are based on a Middle Kingdom nome list. Some nomes had more than one capital town during their history. In others the site of the capital is uncertain.

► Lower Egypt was divided into 20 nomes. This map is based on nome lists in temples of the Greek and Roman (Greco-Roman) periods. Nome boundaries in the Delta were formed by the branches of the Nile.

► A nomarch, seated, oversees the cattle census. Cattle are driven past a kiosk to be counted and recorded by the scribes. The owners are then told how much tax they have to pay.

Mediterranean Sea

Alexandria (Alexandria)

Rosetta Branch

Damietta Branch

Nile

6

12

17

el-Balamun

Tell el-Farain (Buto)

7

5

Sakha (Xois)

Samannud (Sebennytos)

15

16

19

Damanhur (Hermopolis Parva)

Sa el-Hagar (Sais)

Tell el-Ruba (Mendes)

San el-Hagar (Tanis)

3

Abusir (Busiris)

el-Baqliya (Hermopolis Parva)

Tell el-Timai (Thmuis)

Tell Nabasha

14

Kom el-Hisn

Tell Abu Sifa (Sile)

Tell el-Muqdam (Leontopolis)

(Pharbaithos)

(Phakussa)

9

11

20

4

Tell Atrib (Athribis)

Tell Basta (Bubastis)

Tell el-Maskhuta (Pithom)

18

Saft el-Hinna (Per-Sopdu)

8

10

13

2

Ausim (Letopolis)

Tell Hisn (Heliopolis)

(Memphis)

1

UPPER EGYPT

FAIYUM

Sakha Modern name
(Sais) Ancient name
■ Nome capital (if known)
● Other settlement
— Nome boundary
9 Nome number
▨ Fertile land

Scale 1 : 1 800 000

0 — 40 km
0 — 30 miles

The Power of Pharaoh

FROM ABOUT 1350 B.C.E. THE KING OF EGYPT was known as pharaoh. The word means "The Great House"—the royal palace. The king had several palaces. He traveled between them on tours of inspection and was supposed to visit each part of the country at least once every two years.

In theory the king had absolute power but in practice he had to govern Egypt through his officials. Finding officials who would be honest and loyal always seems to have been a problem. Some kings led the army in person against foreign enemies or rebels. The king was also head of the legal system. The Egyptians believed that when the world was made out of chaos the Creator also made *maat*, which means order, truth, and justice. The king had to be the champion of *maat* and the enemy of chaos.

Divine kings

Egyptian kings were thought to get their authority from the gods and to be in some ways godlike or divine themselves. During his lifetime the king was identified with the hawk god Horus who overcame the evil god Set. In his role as high priest, the king was expected to build temples for the gods and to keep them happy with gifts and sacrifices.

▼ A king taking part in the daily temple ritual. He opens a gilded shrine and makes offerings to a statue of the god Amon. The chief offering is a figurine of the goddess who represents *maat*. This symbolizes the king's duty to uphold truth, justice, and order. On the table are vegetables, fruits, and joints of meat offered as a meal for the god. On the circular stand in front of the shrine incense was burned to fill the sanctuary with scented smoke. The priestess (center right) shakes a sacred rattle called a sistrum.

Much of the king's time was taken up with holding elaborate ceremonies that were believed to ensure the well-being of Egypt. The king was thought to be responsible for making the Nile rise to the right level (a "good" Nile) and causing the crops to grow.

One of the most important royal ceremonies was the Sed festival, which was first celebrated in the 30th year of a king's reign. The purpose of the festival, which included a ritual race, was to persuade the gods to renew the king's strength and to grant him a long life.

Royal burials

The king would prepare for his death by building himself a splendid tomb and a temple in which his spirit, or *ka*, would be worshiped as a god. In death, the king was identified with the god Osiris.

According to Egyptian myth, Osiris was murdered by his brother Set but he came back to life to rule over the spirits of the dead. In early times the Egyptians believed that everyone's chance of a life after death depended on the dead king being accepted among the gods. Loyal officials were honored with the right to build their own tombs close to a royal burial place.

▲ A relief of King Sekhemkhet, from copper mines in Sinai, about 2605 B.C.E. This rock carving was discovered in 1973.

◄ In this granite statue King Ramesses II is shown as a handsome young man wearing the Blue Crown. He holds a crook to show that he is the shepherd of his people. On the crown is an *uraeus*, an image of the cobra goddess spitting fire at the enemies of Egypt.

▼ King Senwosret I runs the Sed festival race. He is carrying a sacred oar and a *hepet*—perhaps part of a ship's steering gear—and he is wearing the Red Crown of Lower Egypt.

Rulers of Egypt

THE EGYPTIANS BELIEVED THAT A PERSON'S life was bound up in his or her name. You could help the dead by speaking their names aloud or you could destroy them by erasing their names wherever they appeared. Each Egyptian king had at least five names. The most important were the throne name and the birth name.

Throne names such as Menkheperre (meaning "enduring like the forms of Ra") were taken at a king's coronation. Birth names such as Amonhotep (meaning "Amon is gracious") were family names that were used from childhood.

These two names were usually written inside a cartouche, which was an oval of rope symbolizing "everything which the Sun encircles." By putting their cartouches on objects, Egyptian kings were claiming to rule the world.

Narmer   Aha   Den   Peribsen   Khasekhemwy   Djoser   Snofru

Khufu   Sahura   Wenis   Pepy II   Mentuhotep   Amenemhet I

Senwosret I   Senwosret II   Neferhotep I   Apophis   Tao

▲ The names of the first kings were written inside an oblong panel called a *serekh*. Later royal names use pairs of oval panels.

◀ Queen Nefertiti (also known as Neferneferuaten) was the chief wife of the Pharaoh Akhenaten who ruled Egypt in the 14th century B.C.E. She was famed throughout the ancient world for her outstanding beauty.

▶ A royal pair of the third century B.C.E., Ptolemy II and Arsinoe II. Brother and sister, they were also husband and wife. Though Macedonian by birth, they are shown in Egyptian royal dress.

◄ A typical full royal name in hieroglyphics: "Horus, Mighty Bull, full of glorious appearances, [under the protection of] the Two Ladies, enduring of kingship like Atum, Golden Horus, Strong of Arm, Defeater of the Nine Bows, He of the Sedge and the Bee, Menkheperre, Son of Ra, Thutmose (IV), beloved of Amon-Ra, given life like Ra."

▼ Royal names became more complicated in the later dynasties and Ptolemaic Period. In the bottom row are Egyptian names and titles of some Roman emperors.

Ahmose   Thutmose III   Hatshepsut   Amonhotep III   Akhenaten (Amonhotep IV)

Seti I   Ramesses II   Ramesses III   Ramesses IX   Psusennes I

Shoshenq I   Piye   Taharqa   Psammetichus I   Amasis

Darius   Nectanebo II   Ptolemy I (Soter)   Ptolemy IV (Philopator)   Ptolemy XII (Auletes)

Cleopatra VII (Philopator)   Augustus   Domitian   Trajan   Septimius Severus

Egyptian history is divided into dynasties, groups of rulers that are usually related by birth or marriage. An Egyptian king always had a chief queen who was known as the Great Royal Wife. He might also have a large number of less important wives who made up the royal harem. The Great Royal Wife was often the king's full or half-sister. The ancient Egyptians had no law against marriage between close relatives, but such marriages seem to have been common only among royalty (see also pages 48–49).

How kings were chosen

The crown prince was usually the eldest son of the king and his chief queen. If the Great Royal Wife had no son, an heir had to be chosen from among the children of the lesser wives. There seems to have been no clear rule about how this was to be done. Sometimes the Egyptian gods are said to have made the choice of crown prince.

One story tells how a prince fell asleep close to the Great Sphinx at Giza. The sphinx god appeared to the prince in a dream and complained that the desert sand had almost covered its body. The Sphinx promised that if the prince got the sand cleared away he would become ruler of Egypt. The prince did as he was asked and later became King Thutmose IV. Sometimes an important person of non-royal birth became ruler of Egypt by marrying the eldest daughter of a king and his chief queen.

The coronation of pharaoh

It seems to have been the ritual of the coronation, rather than royal blood, that was thought to give a king divine power. In the coronation ceremony the king was transformed into a god by means of his union with the royal *ka*, or spirit. He was crowned with the Double Crown—the White Crown of Upper Egypt and the Red Crown of Lower Egypt.

His costume included other symbols of his power. For example, he wore a bull's tail attached to his kilt to show that he had the strength of a mighty bull. Egyptian men were usually clean-shaven but the king wore a false beard to imitate the lapis lazuli beards of the gods.

Royal jewelry often included images of the "Two Ladies," the vulture goddess of the south and the cobra goddess of the north.

Everything about the king was intended to project the image of a god here on earth. In practice, a king's status varied from period to period. Some rulers were more successful at claiming divinity than others.

The Gods of Egypt

THE EGYPTIANS TOLD MANY STORIES ABOUT the creation of the world. Most of them start by imagining a time when nothing existed except the Waters of Chaos. In some stories the first thing to emerge from the waters is a blue lotus whose petals hide the infant sun god. Others start with the Primeval Mound, the first dry land, rising above the waters. To the mound comes a phoenix or a hawk, or a goose called the Great Cackler, who lays the world egg.

In another version a creator god exists in the dark waters of chaos for countless ages before realizing that he is lonely. "With the thoughts of his heart and the words of his mouth" the Creator made gods and goddesses. Next he created a world with Egypt at its center. The first people were formed from the tears of the Creator. The Creator is sometimes identified with the sun god and sometimes with other important gods such as Ptah or Amon. Another story attributes the creation of the world to the ram-god Khnum, who made the universe on his potter's wheel.

Egyptian gods and goddesses (deities) were all forms of the Creator but they took on identities of

▲ Questions about when to sow seed are put to the gods Sobek and Isis.

their own. Some had special areas of interest. For example, Thoth was god of wisdom and writing, while Hathor was goddess of love and death.

Strange and sacred creatures

Deities could be shown in full human or animal-headed human form. They often wear distinctive headdresses and carry sacred symbols such as the *ankh* (the sign of life). Some deities had several forms. The god Sobek could appear as a crocodile or as a man with the head of a crocodile. The goddess Hathor might be shown as a beautiful woman, as the head of a woman with cow's ears, as a cow, or as a cow-headed woman. The sun god had numerous forms, some of them worshiped as separate gods. The rising sun was Khepri, shown as a scarab-beetle, the noonday sun was Horus, the hawk god, and the setting sun was Atum, shown as a ram-headed man.

Late in Egyptian history the cult of sacred animals became very important. Creatures such as the ibises sacred to Thoth or the crocodiles sacred to Sobek lived in temples and were given elaborate burials when they died.

1   2   3   4   5   6   7

▶ Granite statue of the god Horus as a crowned hawk, one of three still guarding entrances in the temple of Horus at Edfu. Real hawks were kept in a nearby grove. Every year one of these birds was chosen to be a living divine image in the temple of the Sacred Hawk, which once stood near the main temple.

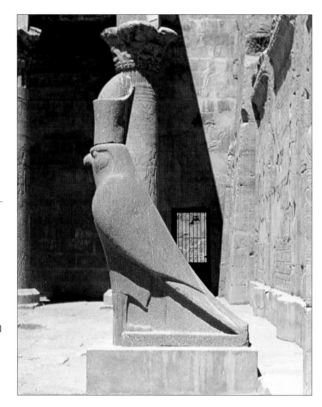

◀ ▶ Human and semihuman forms of some of the chief Egyptian deities:
1 Horus, son of Osiris, a sky god closely linked with the king.
2 Set, enemy of Horus and Osiris, god of storms.
3 Thoth, a moon deity and god of writing, counting, and wisdom.
4 Khnum, a ram god who shapes men and their *kas* on his potter's wheel.
5 Hathor, goddess of love, birth, and death.
6 Sobek, the crocodile god, Lord of the Faiyum.
7 Ra, the sun god in his many forms.
8 Amon, a creator god often linked with Ra.
9 Ptah, another creator god and the patron of craftsmen.
10 Anubis, god of mummification.
11 Osiris, god of agriculture and ruler of the dead.
12 Isis, wife of Osiris, mother of Horus and Mistress of Magic.

Egyptian temples

A temple was the palace of the deity who lived in the cult statue. The statue was hidden inside a shrine in the sanctuary, the holiest part of the temple. Every morning the chief priest entered the sanctuary and opened the shrine. Many rituals were performed, including clothing and perfuming the statue and presenting a meal. In return for these offerings the gods were asked to keep Egypt safe and prosperous.

Ordinary people could not watch the daily ritual but they did join in festivals. On these occasions divine statues were carried outside the temple so the gods might "speak" to the people. The larger temples contained bakeries, butcher shops, breweries, and grainstores to take care of the needs of the god and his human servants. Some temples were centers of learning and artists and craftsmen made a wide range of goods in temple workshops.

The major temples were state-controlled, so the goods were distributed by the government. Kings gave estates, ships, and slaves to support temples. In the 12th century B.C.E. the temple of Amon at Karnak had more than 100,000 people working for it.

8   9   10   11   12

Scribes and Writing

BEING ABLE TO READ AND WRITE WAS essential for anyone wishing to have a career in the Egyptian civil service. Not much is known about Egyptian schools. Some temples ran schools but many boys seem to have studied with local scribes (trained writers).

Reading, writing, and mathematics were the basic subjects. Pupils learned by copying out texts in the two main scripts, hieroglyphic and hieratic. They wrote with pens made from reeds on wooden tablets, pieces of pottery, or scraps of papyrus. Surviving school texts show pupils' spelling mistakes and teachers' corrections. Discipline was strict: "A boy's ear is in his back, he listens when he is beaten."

Be a scribe!

Some of the texts that boys were made to copy out were about the advantages of being a scribe. They stress that scribes sit in the shade and watch while other people do the hard work. Wealth and success are promised to the good pupil. The texts conclude: "If you have any sense, you will be a scribe!"

Scribes were employed to write official or private letters and to draw up legal documents. Other common tasks they undertook were recording the progress of all kinds of work and making lists of goods. Educated people read for pleasure, so scribes wrote or copied out literature such as proverbs, stories, and love poems.

▲ This hieroglyph shows scribal equipment: a palette with red and black ink, a water pot, and a papyrus smoother.

◀ A scribe's palette, from about 1800 B.C.E., with four cakes of ink and a slot to hold reed pens.

▲ A letter written on papyrus. It dates to about 2002 B.C.E. The intact seal at the bottom shows that the letter never reached its destination. The name of the official it was meant for is written in hieratic. The same name written in hieroglyphic is shown alongside.

▲ The Egyptians invented writing paper. This paper was made from the pith of *Cyperus papyrus*, a common marsh plant. The tall stems were cut down and carried off in bundles.

▲ Each stem was stripped of its rind and cut into short pieces. These pieces were then cut lengthwise into narrow strips. It was essential to keep the papyrus pith moist during the process.

▲ ▶ Two layers of strips at right angles were put on a hard surface and beaten until they fused. The papyrus sheets were polished and then glued together to make scrolls for writing on.

◀ The hieroglyphic script at its most beautiful. These painted hieroglyphs are in a Theban tomb of c.1450 B.C.E. The text, written in columns reading from right to left, tells how the owner enjoyed hunting.

Hieroglyphic and other scripts

The hieroglyphic script was used mainly for royal or religious texts carved in stone. Simplified (cursive) hieroglyphs were used for writing religious texts on papyrus.

Letters, records, textbooks, and literature were written in hieratic, a kind of shorthand hieroglyphic. In the seventh century B.C.E. an even more abbreviated script called demotic was introduced.

The hieroglyphic script has about 750 signs. Most of them are pictures of people, animals, plants, or objects. There are two main types of sign—sound signs and sense signs. Sound signs can represent from one to four consonants. The vowels were not written out. A sense sign can be used to write a word or placed after a word to show the area of meaning. For example, verbs of motion have a pair of legs attached to the signs.

▲ The Rosetta Stone dates to 196 B.C.E. It is inscribed with a royal decree written in Egyptian in two different scripts, hieroglyphic and demotic, and in Greek. This helped the French scholar J-F. Champollion to decipher the hieroglyphic script.

One consonant						
Y	W	F	M	N	R	T

Two consonant						
HR	WR	WN	GM	HM	NB	D3

Three consonant						
HPR	D'M	NTR	'NH	HNT	W3D	WSR

◀ ▶ A typical sentence in ancient Egyptian and a selection of sound signs and sense signs: "His Majesty set out on a chariot of gold."

This sentence is taken from the Battle Annals of Thutmose III (see page 41). The transcription underneath shows which sound signs are written by the hieroglyphs. The English translation below that follows the Egyptian word order. There are no breaks between words in Egyptian scripts. Marks under letters indicate pronunciation.

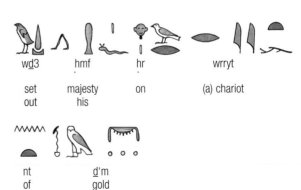

wd3	hmf	hr		wrryt
set out	majesty his	on		(a) chariot

nt		d'm	
of		gold	

Sense signs				
Nose/ joy	Precious metal	Wood	Motion	Woman/ female

Burial Customs

THE ANCIENT EGYPTIANS TOOK MANY precautions to make sure that the spirits of the dead could enjoy a life after death. Those who could afford them had elaborate family tombs.

People visited these tombs to make regular food offerings to their dead relations. In case the family neglected this duty, stone stelae (carved gravestones) were placed in the outer areas of tombs. These often show the dead person sitting next to a table of food offerings. They are inscribed with a magical formula. The idea was that when this was spoken aloud the dead got everything they needed to live on.

The Book of the Dead

Before the dead could reach the paradise known as the Field of Reeds they had to pass through an underworld full of monsters and demons. In the Middle Kingdom some coffins were painted with maps of the underworld and with spells against its dangers. In the New Kingdom the spells were written on papyrus scrolls and placed in the tomb.

One spell collection known as the Book of the Dead stresses that all spirits were judged before Osiris. The dead person's heart was weighed against a feather representing *maat* (truth). If their heart was heavier than truth because they had led a wicked life they would be eaten by a monster and die a second death. Those who passed the judgment became blessed spirits who lived with the gods. Such spirits were still believed to want intact bodies to return to.

In early times burial in hot dry sand preserved bodies naturally. When coffins came into use some artificial way of stopping decay was needed. At some periods the process of mummification was used to preserve bodies.

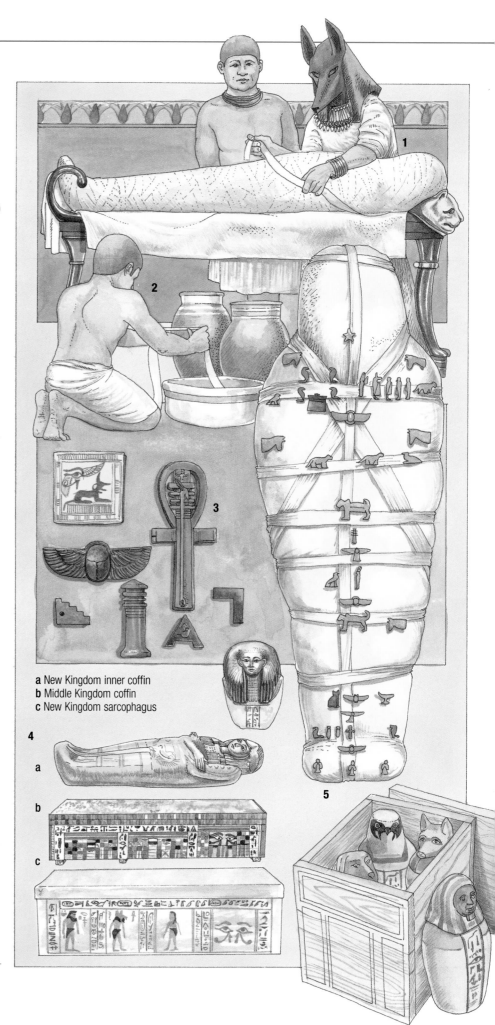

a New Kingdom inner coffin
b Middle Kingdom coffin
c New Kingdom sarcophagus

▶ Embalmers and burial equipment.

1 Wrapping a mummy. The chief embalmer wears a jackal mask to impersonate Anubis, protector of the dead.

2 Spells were recited as each part of the mummy was separately wrapped in long strips of linen. A shroud might then be tied over the whole mummy.

3 Amulets were placed in the layers of wrappings to protect each body part.

4 In rich burials the mummy lay in a set of cartonnage coffins inside a stone sarcophagus. Cartonnage was made by soaking linen or papyrus layers in plaster.

5 The liver, lungs, stomach, and intestines were packed into jars and placed near the coffin.

Mummification

The exact treatment of the body depended on what the family was able to afford. The most elaborate method took about 70 days. First the embalmers took the brain out through the nose. Next the vital organs, such as the lungs, the liver, and the stomach, were removed and treated separately, although the heart might be left in the chest. The inside of the body was cleaned and packed with scented resins. Natron, a natural drying agent, was put inside and all around the body.

After about 40 days the body would have completely dried out. The next stage was to put packing material under the skin to imitate flesh and to refill the main cavity with scented materials. Finally, the mummy was treated with perfumed oils and molten resin before being wrapped for burial.

▲ An embalmer assembles a set of mummy amulets in a workshop full of funerary equipment. Decorated tombs and coffins were status symbols in ancient Egypt, sometimes given by the king to valued officials. Ordinary people bought the best equipment they could afford to prepare for their own funerals. Personal possessions such as clothes, jewelry, and furniture might also be buried with the dead for use in the afterlife.

▲ The 3,300-year-old head of Seti I. This is the best preserved of all the royal mummies. Egyptian mummies give useful information about the diseases people suffered from in ancient times.

▶ From about 1700 B.C.E. onwards, magical figurines known as *shabtis* were placed in tombs. A *shabti* acted as a substitute for the tomb owner if his spirit was called up to do farm work in the afterlife.

◀ The shrouded mummy of a priestess in her anthropoid (mummy-shaped) coffin. The lid incorporates a mummy mask and painted garlands.

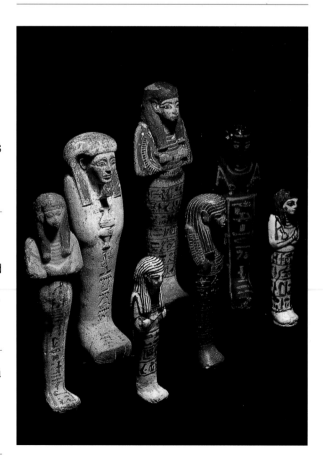

Everyday Life

MOST PEOPLE IN ANCIENT EGYPT WERE employed by the state, which also often provided them with housing. Wages were paid in the form of food, clothing, and other basic necessities. Surplus rations could be swapped for household items and luxuries. These in turn might be exchanged. In one typical transaction a New Kingdom workman bartered two goats, one pig, and two planks of sycamore wood for a decorated coffin.

Food and drink

Bread, beer, vegetables, and a little fresh or dried fish were the predominant items in the diet of the poor. Better-off Egyptians enjoyed dates, pomegranates, and figs. They also ate meat, especially beef and goose, and drank date or grape wine. The decayed teeth found in some mummies suggest that they had a tendency to over-indulge in cakes that were sweetened with honey and fruit.

Clothing and fashion

Most clothes were made of pleated linen. Men dressed in loincloths and kilts and, at some periods, shirts. Women had shawls and narrow ankle-length dresses. Reed or leather sandals might be worn outdoors. Children wore few or no clothes. Boys had all but one side-lock of hair shaved off until they reached puberty.

Adult hairstyles could be very elaborate, and important people owned wigs in a range of lengths and styles, made from human hair or wool. Both sexes wore jewelry and used make-up, especially eye paint. The Egyptians loved perfume, and scented oils were rubbed into the skin.

▶ A tomb scene depicting craftsmen at work. At the top are leatherworkers and men making burial items. In the second row are chariotmakers, sculptors, and carpenters. The third row shows furniture and statues being finished. In the fourth row are metalworkers and boatbuilders.

▼ Left: A child's pull-along wooden horse from the Greco-Roman period. Right: A wooden comb, c.1300 B.C.E., from Kom Medinet Ghurab. Many objects linked with hairdressing and make-up have survived.

◀ Town life in ancient Egypt. Houses were made from mud-brick. The homes of ordinary people were small and built close together. Livestock such as goats and geese might be kept in the middle of towns. Cats, dogs, and monkeys were popular pets. Cooking was done in domed clay ovens in open kitchen yards. The flat roofs were used as storage and work space.

Egypt Before the Pharaohs

THE FIRST INHABITANTS OF EGYPT WERE nomadic hunters and animal herders who lived on the savanna. Gradually people moved down into the Nile valley and adopted a settled way of life that was based on agriculture (see pages 10–11). We know very little about the way these people lived, but there were separate groups with different cultures.

Predynastic Middle and Lower Egypt

Sometime around 5400 B.C.E., one group settled in an area that was centered on the Faiyum, a large lake in the middle of Egypt. This group did grow some crops, but fishing seems to have been vital to their survival. Other groups, known from several large village sites in Lower Egypt, grew corn, hunted desert animals, and fished.

At Merimda Beni Salama, the earliest of the northern sites, people lived in clusters of reed huts. They used stone tools, made simple pottery, and spun cloth. At the later site of Ma'adi there is evidence that people were occupied in farming, herding, and metalworking.

Predynastic Upper Egypt

In the south the Badarian/Tasian culture spread along the Nile valley. These people lived in small villages on the floodplain and buried their dead with grave goods in cemeteries on the edge of the desert. This suggests that they practiced a religion with a belief in an afterlife. Items found in Badarian/Tasian graves include decorated pots, bead necklaces, linen clothing, clay figurines of people and animals, amulets, ivory spoons, and combs.

Descended from the Badarian/Tasian people was the Naqada I (or Amratian) culture. Metal was still rare but stoneworking was highly skilled. Flint was worked into rippled knives and arrowheads and harder stones were made into clubs. These weapons would have been used for hunting the desert animals that were an important source of food. They may also indicate a more warlike society.

In the Naqada II (or Gerzean) Period people lived in large tribal communities that were probably often warring. Some burials contain much richer grave goods than average, for example, gold and lapis lazuli jewelry, elaborate slate palettes used for grinding eye paint, and beautiful ivory combs and knife handles. This provides evidence of a wealthy ruling class at this time.

▼ A 15-in- (38-cm-) tall basalt statue from Naqada, probably from the late Predynastic Period. This fine piece shows that the Egyptians had already mastered the art of carving in hard stone.

▼ Clay figure of a roaring hippopotamus taken from a Naqada II grave at Hiw. Hippopotamuses would have been a common danger in the Nile River at this period. Hippopotamus hunts are shown on Predynastic pottery, and hippopotamus tusks were carved into figurines and pendants.

◄ A crude clay figurine of a woman, from a tomb of the Naqada I Period. The exaggerated thighs and legs imply that the figurine was a fertility charm.

Trade in the Predynastic Period

By the Naqada III Period all of Upper Egypt was ruled by a line of chieftains who called themselves kings. These kings are sometimes known as Dynasty O.

A few Naqada III objects are decorated with motifs borrowed from the art of Mesopotamia (modern Iraq), where a sophisticated urban society existed. Archaeologists used to believe that the rapid changes that took place at the end of the Predynastic Period were caused by foreigners invading from the east and seizing power. There is no strong evidence for an invasion, but the Egyptians were certainly trading goods and ideas with the peoples to the east.

It was probably at this time that the Upper Egyptians began mining and exporting gold. The important early town of Ombos, near Naqada, was close to a major gold mining area.

Major Predynastic and Early Dynastic sites

All dates given for the Predynastic cultures are uncertain. The cultures of Upper and Lower Egypt cannot easily be related in their development.

1 Badarian/Tasian sites c.4500–4000 B.C.E.

2 Naqada I sites c.4000–3500 B.C.E.

3 Naqada II sites c.3500–3000 B.C.E.

4 Lower Egypt cultures sites c.4800–3000 B.C.E.

5 Faiyum culture sites c.5400–4400 B.C.E.

6 Naqada III and Early Dynastic sites c.3200–2575 B.C.E.

▲ A Naqada I red-ware pot decorated with desert animals, a frequent theme in the art of this period. The tombs near Naqada were excavated in 1895.

▶ Predynastic and Early Dynastic Egypt. Most of the major Predynastic sites are on the margins of the desert. By Early Dynastic times many of these sites had been abandoned and new settlements were founded on the Nile's floodplain. In this period Nubia was inhabited by a people whom historians call the "A-Group."

29

The First Pyramid Builders

ACCORDING TO EGYPTIAN LEGEND, THE country was first united under King Menes. Menes is said to have been a king of Upper Egypt who conquered Lower Egypt and founded a new capital at Memphis. Two early kings called Narmer and Aha, whose tombs were found in the sacred city of Abydos, have each been identified as Menes. Events from the reigns of both kings may have contributed to the legend of Menes and the founding of the First Dynasty.

Early Dynastic Egypt

During the First Dynasty the use of hieroglyphic writing became widespread. Recent finds have shown that this unique pictorial script (see pages 22–23) is probably the oldest form of writing in the world.

Towns of some size began to be established, and brick buildings replaced reed huts. Brick *mastaba* tombs were built for high officials at Saqqara, the cemetery for Memphis. Inside these large rectangular flat-topped tombs, close to the burial chamber, were storerooms full of goods. Stone stelae were set up against one wall of the *mastaba* tomb at the place where offerings were made to the dead. When a ruler of this period died, some of his servants were killed and buried near him so that their spirits could continue to serve him in the afterlife.

Little is known about the history of Early Dynastic Egypt. During the Second Dynasty there seems to

have been a civil war between two kings, Peribsen and Khasekhemwy. These kings were followers of the rival gods Set and Horus. The victor, Khasekhemwy, included both gods in the writing of his full name (see page 18), perhaps as a gesture towards peace.

Khasekhemwy is the earliest Egyptian king for whom we have a stone statue. All the royal tombs of the First and Second Dynasties have been robbed, but the few objects that survive are very fine. Among them are four bracelets of gold, lapis lazuli, and turquoise found in the tomb of King Djer at Abydos, on an arm torn from a mummy by tomb raiders.

Imhotep and the Step Pyramid

The reign of King Djoser in the Third Dynasty was later remembered as a golden age of wisdom. Among

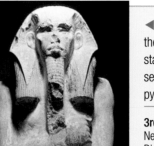

◄ King Djoser, who built the Step Pyramid. This statue was found in a sealed chamber near the pyramid's northeast corner.

▼ Limestone gaming disk decorated with a pair of owls. This disk is one of a set of 45 found in the tomb of a First-Dynasty official. Board games were a popular pastime.

▲ The restored southeast entrance to the Step Pyramid complex at Saqqara. These stone walls imitate the paneled brick of palaces of this period. Inside the enclosure was an area dedicated to Sed festivals (see page 16) at which King Djoser could gain eternal life and power.

Djoser's officials was Imhotep, the first genius known to history. Imhotep is said to have written books on medicine and was later worshiped by Egyptians as a god of healing.

Tradition also named Imhotep as the inventor of stone architecture and the designer of Egypt's first pyramid—the Step Pyramid at Saqqara, built for King Djoser. Imhotep's name has been found inside the Step Pyramid enclosure, so it is likely that he was the chief architect of this extraordinary group of stone buildings. The pyramid began as a normal *mastaba*. Later, more *mastabas* were added on top, until it consisted of six terraces, or steps, and was 200 feet (60 m) high. The surface was originally encased in smooth white limestone.

Like the later pyramids (see pages 86–87), the Step Pyramid complex was both a royal tomb and a temple where the spirit, or *ka*, of the dead king could be worshiped. Parts of it are stone versions of the temporary reed shrines of the Sed festivals. The effort and cost that went into building the Step Pyramid shows the importance of the cult of the divine king.

▼ The Step Pyramid at Saqqara—the first pyramid to be built—was begun in about 2630 B.C.E., making it the oldest stone structure of its size in the world. Under the pyramid is Djoser's tomb. It was robbed in ancient times, and the granite sarcophagus found to be empty.

▶ The architect of the Step Pyramid began with a large *mastaba* tomb **1**, but then had the idea of building a pyramid in steps. The pyramid increased in size several times **2–3**, until the finished structure had six steps and was 200 ft (60 m) high **4**. Changes were made in the design of the substructure when underground tombs were added for other royal family members.

The Old Kingdom

SNOFRU, THE FIRST KING OF THE FOURTH Dynasty, built at least two true (straight-sided) pyramids for himself. One of them is known as the "Bent Pyramid" because halfway up its height it changes angle sharply.

During the Fourth Dynasty the most important government posts were held by members of the royal family. In Snofru's reign the Egyptians built a fortified town at Buhen in Nubia. From here they could exploit the Nubian gold fields and control trade routes into Africa.

Snofru was reputed to be a kindly ruler. In contrast, Khufu (Cheops), the builder of the Great Pyramid at Giza, was long remembered as a cruel tyrant. Khephren and Menkaura also built vast pyramids at Giza.

The tombs of queens, princesses, and high officials were grouped around the pyramids. Human sacrifice (see page 30) no longer had any part in the royal burial rites. Statues of Fourth Dynasty kings show them as serene figures, confident in their power over Egypt and in their status as living gods. This may be misleading, as the brief reigns of some Old Kingdom rulers suggest conflicts we know little about.

The Old Kingdom was a high point as far as Egyptian art was concerned. Wonderful statues and reliefs were carved in stone. Mathematics, astronomy, and engineering also flourished during this time. The challenge of pyramid building may have been the driving force behind these artistic and scientific advances.

Pyramid building—the workforce

The pyramids were built by a permanent workforce of craftsmen and by peasants who were called up to work on royal projects during the months when the fields were flooded. As many as 100,000 men may have labored over 20 flood seasons to build each pyramid. Building projects on such a gigantic scale needed a stable and prosperous country and a genius for organization. The huge civil service developed to cope with pyramid building remained a key feature of Egyptian civilization.

The Fifth-Dynasty pyramids were smaller in scale than earlier pyramids, but several kings of this dynasty also built magnificent stone temples for the sun god Ra. The pyramid of Wenis, the last king of the Fifth Dynasty, was the first to be inscribed with the famous spells known as the Pyramid Texts. These spells helped the king become a god in the afterlife and take his place among the stars.

▶ King Menkaura with the goddesses Hathor and Bat.

**Selected kings 2—
Old Kingdom
2575–2134 B.C.E.**

4th Dynasty 2575–2465
Snofru 2575–2551
Khufu (Cheops) 2551–2528
Djedefra 2528–2520
Khephren 2520–2494
Menkaura 2490–2472
Shepseskaf 2472–2467
5th Dynasty 2465–2323
Userkaf 2465–2458
Sahura 2458–2446
Neferirkara 2446–2426
Shepseskara 2426–2419
Raneferef 2419–2416
Neuserra 2416–2392
Menkauhor 2396–2388
Djedkara 2388–2356
Wenis 2356–2323
6th Dynasty 2323–2150
Teti 2323–2291
Pepy I 2289–2255
Merenra 2255–2246
Pepy II 2246–2152
**7th/8th Dynasties
2150–2134**
Numerous kings.

**First Intermediate Period
2134–2040 B.C.E.**

9th/10th Dynasties 2134–2040
Kings ruling from
Herakleopolis—Ity, Merykara,
Khety.

11th Dynasty 2134–2040
Kings ruling from Thebes,
including:
Inyotef I 2134–2118
Inyotef II 2118–2069
Inyotef III 2069–2061
Nebhepetra Mentuhotep
2061–2010

▼ A wooden statue of a Sixth-Dynasty "Chief of the Royal Farmers."

▼ Painted limestone statue from Saqqara. Important people were often shown as scribes with papyrus rolls on their laps.

Mediterranean Sea

LOWER EGYPT

Tell el-Ruba (Mendes)

Abu Rawash
Tell Hisn (Heliopolis)
Abu Ghurab
Giza
(Memphis)
Abusir
Saqqara
Dahshur
Maidum
MIDDLE
Ihnasya el-Medina
Dishasha
(Herakleopolis)
Wadi el-Sheikh
EGYPT

Bahariya
Oasis

Gebel el-Teir

Beni Hasan

Meir (Cusae)
Deir el-Gabrawi
Asyut (Lykopolis)
Qaw el-Kebir (Antaeopolis)

UPPER   EGYPT

Nag el-Deir
(Abydos)
Nile
Dendara (Iunet)
Wadi Hammamat

Dakhla Oasis
Balat

el-Kharga
Oasis

Luxor
(Thebes)
Gebelein (Per-Hathor)
el-Moalla
Kom el-Ahmar
(Hierakonpolis)
Mueilha

Gebel el-Hammam
Hagar el-Gharb
Aswan (Elephantine)
EGYPT
NUBIA
Kurkur
Oasis

Dunqul
Oasis

Tumas

Tushka

LOWER
NUBIA
(Buhen)

Salima
Oasis

UPPER
NUBIA
Kulb

Wadi Kharit
Wadi Maghara

SINAI

Red Sea

Aswan Modern name
(Buhen) Ancient name
▨ Fertile land
- - - Trade route
■ Capital city
● Settlement or site

Types of site
▲ Papyrus
● Graffiti
■ Decorated tomb
◆ Other

Scale 1 : 5 000 000
0   100 km
0   75 miles

Old Kingdom and First Intermediate Period

Papyrus sites Papyrus was probably first used for writing on in the Old Kingdom. Old Kingdom papyri include legal documents and temple records.

Graffiti sites These consist of names and titles scratched on rocks by members of Egyptian mining and trading expeditions. Most date from the Sixth Dynasty.

Decorated tomb sites By the late Old Kingdom important officials were building themselves elaborate tombs in provincial cemeteries. This shows the increasing wealth and independence of the regions. The decoration in First Intermediate Period tombs is crude compared with Old Kingdom art.

Rise of the nomarchs

The Sixth Dynasty brought a decline in royal power. The government was now no longer dominated by princes. In their wonderfully decorated tombs great officials hid their importance behind humble titles such as "Keeper of the King's Nail Clippings."

In theory all the land in Egypt belonged to the king but over time estates were given away to support temples and to reward officials. Such estates could be registered as belonging to the cults of gods or dead ancestors. This meant that little or no tax was payable on the produce of the estates, and so the wealth of the king was reduced. The central government was also threatened by the gradual rise in power of the nomarchs (see pages 14–15). The office of nomarch had begun to pass within families from father to son.

The slide into chaos

The Sixth Dynasty effectively ended with Pepy II, who came to the throne as a small child and reigned for more than 90 years. A series of low Niles caused famines, some nomarchs declared themselves kings, and Egypt became divided into a number of feudal states. The country began to suffer what it feared most—chaos. For many, the First Intermediate Period was a time of poverty and violence. The country's sufferings when central government failed became a common theme for later Egyptian writers: "All happiness has disappeared, the land is bowed down in misery." (13th-Dynasty poem).

◀ Egypt and Nubia in the Old Kingdom and the First Intermediate Period. The major Fourth- and Fifth-Dynasty sites are clustered near the capital, Memphis. Lower Nubia was almost uninhabited until it was settled by the "C-Group" during the Sixth Dynasty.

The Middle Kingdom

IN 2040 B.C.E. EGYPT WAS REUNITED BY A KING from Thebes, Nebhepetra Mentuhotep. The country soon prospered and large-scale building works began again. After two more Theban kings a new dynasty, the 12th, was founded by the vizier Amenemhet. We do not know whether this transfer of power was peaceful or violent.

Amenemhet built a new capital city called Itjtawy somewhere near el-Lisht. This gave him more central control. He reorganized the country's administration, keeping the nomarchs who had supported him but taking away power from the regional governors. After 20 years he made his son Senwosret co-ruler, an action copied by some later 12th-Dynasty kings. Amenemhet seems to have been murdered while Senwosret was away fighting the Libyans, but there was no collapse of order. Under Amenemhet and Senwosret Egypt expanded into Nubia again and a long chain of forts was built along the Nile there.

The careworn kings

The greatest 12th-Dynasty king was Senwosret III. He conquered more of Nubia than the Egyptians had ever controlled before. Egyptian influence spread into Palestine. He also increased the power of the central government, at the expense of the nomarchs.

The pyramids of most 12th-Dynasty rulers were shoddily built but the art of this period is of a very high quality. Statues of Senwosret III and his son Amenemhet III show them with grim age-worn faces. They seem far more human than the god-kings of the previous era. Middle Kingdom literature, too, stresses the cares and problems of kingship.

Selected kings 3—
Middle Kingdom
2040–1640 B.C.E.

11th Dynasty 2040–1991
Nebhepetra Mentuhotep II
  2061–2010
Mentuhotep III 2010–1998
Mentuhotep IV 1998–1991
12th Dynasty 1991–1783
Amenemhet I 1991–1962
Senwosret I 1971–1926
Amenemhet II 1929–1892
Senwosret II 1897–1878
Senwosret III 1878–1841
Amenemhet III 1844–1797
Amenemhet IV 1799–1787
Queen Nefrusobek
  1787–1783
13th Dynasty 1783–1640
About 70 kings, most with
short reigns. Among the best
known are:

Sobekhotep I c.1750
Hor c.1748?
Sobekhotep III c.1745
Neferhotep I c.1741–1730
Sobekhotep IV c.1730–1720
Sobekhotep V c.1720–1715
Aya c.1704–1690

◀ Black basalt figure of King Neferhotep I.

**Second Intermediate Period
1640–1550 B.C.E.**

14th Dynasty
Minor kings contemporary with
Dynasties 13 and 15.
15th Dynasty 1640–1532
Hyksos kings ruling from Avaris:
Salitis
Sheshi
Khian
Apophis c.1585–1542
Khamudi c.1542–1532
16th Dynasty
Minor Hyksos kings
contemporary with 15th Dynasty.
17th Dynasty 1640–1550
Numerous Theban kings. The
best known are:
Inyotef V c.1640–1635
Seqenenra c.1560–1555
Kamose 1555–1550

▼ Granite sphinx with the grim face of Amenemhet III. The sphinx was a part-human, part-lion monster that traditionally protected Egypt from its enemies. Several later kings inscribed their names on this awe-inspiring statue.

◀ A beautifully carved granite obelisk at Heliopolis from the time of Senwosret I. Obelisks were sacred to the sun god. Not much stone architecture survives from the Middle Kingdom.

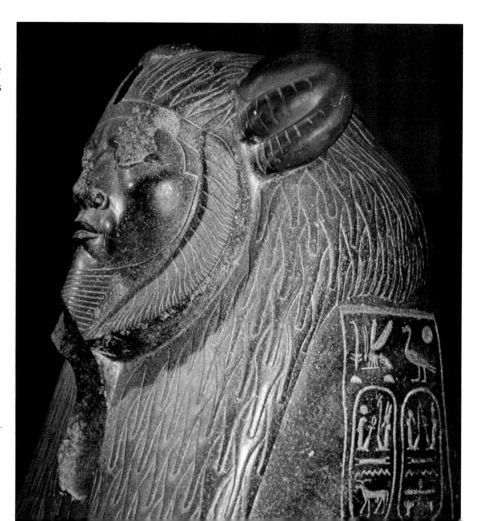

The reign of the Hyksos

The 12th Dynasty ended with a queen, so the royal family had probably died out. Egypt continued to prosper in the 13th Dynasty but most kings seem to have reigned only for a few years. It is possible that real power was in the hands of officials such as the vizier. In time, rival dynasties emerged. One of these, the 15th, were foreigners known as the Hyksos.

The Hyksos people had entered Egypt through Palestine and settled in the Delta. They established their own communities and lived by their own laws. The Hyksos kings managed to assert their power over the whole of Egypt. They also made an alliance with Kush, an area of Upper Nubia ruled by local princes.

During what is known as the Second Intermediate Period, local rulers were tolerated as long as they paid tribute to the Hyksos kings at their capital, Avaris. A new dynasty of Theban kings arose in the south. At first these 17th-Dynasty kings had to pay tribute to the Hyksos, but their aim was to free Egypt from foreign control.

King Seqenenra led an army against the Hyksos but the terrible ax wounds on his mummy show that he died after a battle. His successor, Kamose, continued the struggle, fighting the Hyksos and the Nubians of Kush.

▶ Egypt and Nubia in the Middle Kingdom and the Second Intermediate Period. The map shows capital cities and changing centers of power during the 11th to 17th Dynasties. These include areas of Nubia controlled by Egypt's line of forts along the Nile, and major sites of the Nubian culture groups.

Middle Kingdom and Second Intermediate Period

Find spots The finds include bronze weapons and distinctive pottery of the Middle Bronze Age culture of Palestine and those parts of Egypt settled by the Hyksos.

Dynasty capitals The centers of power often changed with dynasties. The local god of a dynastic capital then became an important deity.

"Pan-grave" sites The "Pan-grave" people were nomads from the Eastern Desert who served as mercenary soldiers in Egypt and Nubia.

12th-Dynasty forts and "C-group" settlements The Egyptians built forts to control the "C-group" culture people of Lower Nubia and to create a buffer zone against the fierce "Kerma culture" people of Kush (Upper Nubia). In the Second Intermediate Period the Princes of Kush ruled Lower Nubia and attacked Upper Egypt.

(Byblos)

Mediterranean Sea

PALESTINE

LOWER
EGYPT
Sakha (Xois)
14
Kom el-Hisn
Farasha
15
Tell el-Daba (Avaris)
LIBYA
Tell Basta (Bubastis)
Ghita
el-Khatana
Tell Hisn (Heliopolis)
Tell el-Yahudiya (Leontopolis)
12,13 (Memphis)
Qasr el-Sagha
el-Lisht (Itjtawy)
12,13
Sidmant el-Gebel
el-Lahun
Serabit el-Khadim
Wadi Maghara
MIDDLE
EGYPT
SINAI
Nile
Eastern Desert
Bahariya
Oasis
Farafra
Oasis
15TH DYNASTY
17TH DYNASTY
Asyut (Lykopolis)
el-Mustagidda
Deir Rifa
Qaw el-Kebir (Antaeopolis)
UPPER EGYPT
Hiw (Diospolis Parva)
Deir el-Ballas
Red Sea
Dakhla
Oasis
Luxor (Thebes)
11,17
Esna (Latopolis)
el-Kab (Nekheb)
el-Kharga
Oasis
Edfu (Apollinopolis Magna)
EGYPT
17TH DYNASTY
Aswan (Elephantine)
KERMA CULTURE
NUBIA
LOWER NUBIA
Quban
Tumas
Aniba (Miam)
Shablul
Faras
Serra East
(Buhen)
12TH–13TH DYNASTY
KERMA CULTURE
Semna
UPPER
NUBIA
Sai
KUSH
(Kerma Culture)
Kerma

Hiw Modern name
(Xois) Ancient name
Fertile land
Southern Palestine

Egyptian sites
12 ■ Capital city with dynasty number
◆ 12th-Dynasty fort
● Other

Nubian sites
■ Capital city
◆ C-group settlement
● Other

▲ Findspot
▼ "Pan-grave" site

Scale 1 : 7 000 000
0   150 km
0   100 miles

The New Kingdom

HMOSE, FIRST KING OF THE 18TH DYNASTY, finally drove the Hyksos out of Egypt and the Prince of Kush out of Lower Nubia. By the end of his reign Egypt controlled an area reaching from Palestine to Upper Nubia.

Thutmose I led the armies of Egypt farther north than they had ever gone before. He founded an empire in Palestine and Syria.

His successor, Thutmose II, died young. His widow and sister, Hatshepsut, acted as regent for the boy king Thutmose III, her husband's son by a lesser wife. After a few years she declared herself king. Statues show that she wore the traditional clothing of the male pharaohs. Hatshepsut's reign seems to have been peaceful and prosperous. Reliefs in her beautiful temple at Deir el-Bahri depict an expedition returning from Punt (probably present-day Eritrea) with valuable goods such as incense trees.

After Hatshepsut's death, Thutmose III fought many campaigns to secure Egypt's rule in Palestine and Syria. Tribute from the empire and gold from Nubia made Egypt the richest nation in the ancient world. The 18th-Dynasty kings used this wealth to build temples. The most favored god was Amon, whose temple at Karnak in Thebes became the largest in Egypt.

**Selected kings 4—
New Kingdom
1550–1070 B.C.E.**

18th Dynasty 1550–1307
Ahmose 1550–1525
Amonhotep I 1525–1504
Thutmose I 1504–1492
Thutmose II 1492–1479
Thutmose III 1479–1425
Queen Hatshepsut
    1473–1458
Amonhotep II
    1427–1401
Thutmose IV 1401–1391
Amonhotep III
    1391–1353
Amonhotep IV (Akhenaten)
    1353–1335
Smenkhkara 1335–1333

▲ Sphinx with the face of a New Kingdom ruler.

Tutankhamon 1333–1323
Aya 1323–1319
Horemheb 1319–1307

19th Dynasty 1307–1196
Ramesses 1 1307–1306
Seti I 1306–1290
Ramesses II 1290–1224
Merneptah 1224–1214
Seti II 1214–1204
Siptah 1204–1198
Queen Tawosre 1198–1196

20th Dynasty 1196–1070
Sethnakhte 1196–1194
Ramesses III 1194–1163
Ramesses IV 1163–1156
Ramesses V 1156–1151
Ramesses VI 1151–1143
Ramesses VII 1143–1136
Ramesses VIII 1136–1131
Ramesses IX 1131–1112
Ramesses X 1112–1100
Ramesses XI 1100–1070

▼ A riverside scene in the New Kingdom. The *shaduf*, shown lifting water from the river to irrigate an orchard, was a New Kingdom invention. An overseer standing on the bank is dressed in the elaborate costume of this period.

► Egypt and Nubia in the New Kingdom and the early Third Intermediate Period. During the latter period the High Priests of Amon at Thebes controlled the area between Aswan and el-Hiba while the kings of the 21st and 22nd Dynasties ruled the north. The sites marked in Nubia are towns or temples built by the Egyptians during the New Kingdom.

Mediterranean Sea

LOWER EGYPT   PALESTINE

Sa el-Hagar (Sais)
21,22 ■ San el-Hagar (Tanis)
19,20 ■ Tell el-Daba (Pi-Ramesses)
23 ■ Tell el-Muqdam (Leontopolis)
22 ■ Tell Basta (Bubastis)

Saqqara ■ (Memphis) 18,19

MIDDLE EGYPT

Kom Medinet Ghurab
Ihnasya el-Medina (Herakleopolis)

21ST–22ND DYNASTY
HIGH PRIESTS OF AMON

el-Hiba (Ankyronon Polis)

Bahariya Oasis

Serabit el-Khadim

SINAI

el-Ashmunein (Hermopolis)
■ el-Amarna (Akhetaten) 18

Red Sea

Dakhla Oasis

Nile

UPPER   EGYPT

(Abydos)
Dendara (Iunet)
Qift (Koptos)
Deir el-Bahri
Luxor (Thebes) 18

el-Kharga Oasis

el-Kab (Nekheb)
Edfu (Apollinopolis Magna)

EGYPT   Aswan (Elephantine)
NUBIA
Kurkur Oasis
Beit el-Wali
Dunqul Oasis
LOWER NUBIA

Aniba (Miam)
el-Sebua
el-Lessiya
Abu Simbel
Faras
(Buhen)
Mirgissa (Iqen)

Salima Oasis

Kumma

UPPER NUBIA

Sai
Soleb
Sesebi

Qift   Modern name
(Koptos)   Ancient name
▨   Fertile land
18 ■   Egyptian capital city with dynasty number
■   Nubian capital city
●   Other Egyptian site

Scale 1 : 5 000 000
0   100 km
0   75 miles

Capital cities of the New Kingdom and later

Thebes The New Kingdom religious capital and the royal burial place.

Memphis Administrative capital for the majority of the 18th Dynasty and in the early 19th Dynasty.

el-Amarna New capital begun in year 5 of Akhenaten. Abandoned some 15 years later under Tutankhamon.

Pi-Ramesses Built under Ramesses II. The probable site is the Qantir district near Tell el-Daba in the northeast of the Delta.

Tanis Capital and burial place of kings of the 21st and 22nd Dynasties.

Bubastis City of origin and religious capital of the 22nd Dynasty.

Leontopolis Capital and probable burial place of some 23rd-Dynasty rulers.

Akhenaten, the sun king

Amonhotep III built more lavishly than any of his predecessors. Remains of his palace at Thebes show the splendor and luxury of his court. His son, Amonhotep IV, changed his name to Akhenaten and made Aten (the sun disk) the chief deity of Egypt. He began to build a new capital at el-Amarna. Next he declared that Aten was the only god and closed down the temples of all the other deities.

Akhenaten also broke away from tradition by having himself shown in informal family scenes, kissing his beautiful wife Nefertiti (see page 18) or playing with his daughters. Akhenaten's reforms were not popular, however, and in the reign of Tutankhamon the new capital was abandoned and the old religion was restored.

The Ramessid Pharaohs

After Tutankhamon the throne passed to a series of officials. The third was a general, Ramesses, who founded the 19th Dynasty. His son, Seti I, was a forceful ruler. His grandson, Ramesses II, reigned for 66 years and erected more buildings and colossal statues than any other Egyptian king.

Egypt was still prosperous but its borders were under threat. Merneptah, Ramesses II's successor, had to fight off Libyans and other invaders. Ramesses III, the second king of the 20th Dynasty, fought great land and sea battles against a group of invaders known as the Sea Peoples. The 20th Dynasty was a period of slow decline when the power of the priesthood at Thebes began to rival that of the king.

The Near East

THE EGYPTIANS THOUGHT THEMSELVES superior to all other races. Foreigners usually appear in Egyptian art as humble tribute bearers or as bound prisoners. The Nubians to the south, the Libyans to the west, and the "vile Asiatics" to the east were pictured on the king's footstool or on the underside of his sandals to symbolize Egypt trampling on its enemies. In reality some Near Eastern nations were dangerous rivals.

Legacy of the Hyksos

During the late Middle Kingdom large numbers of Asiatics were allowed to settle in Egypt. This seems to have made it easy for the Hyksos kings to seize power (see page 35). The Asiatic immigrants brought new bronzeworking techniques as well as improved types of looms and potter's wheels. They also introduced new kinds of weapons and the practice of fighting from chariots.

The Theban kings of the 17th and 18th Dynasties were not content to drive the Hyksos out of Egypt. They pursued them into Palestine and southern Syria. These areas were divided into small states with ruling princes who could be terrorized into acknowledging the king of Egypt as their overlord and into paying him tribute. Northern Syria, however, was part of the powerful kingdom of Mitanni (Naharin), an Indo-Iranian empire centered on northern Mesopotamia.

Mitanni and the Hittites

Thutmose I attacked Mitanni and led an Egyptian army as far north as the Euphrates River. He proceeded to celebrate his victory with a great elephant hunt at Niya.

To keep control of the empire it had won, Egypt frequently had to send an army to recapture rebel states or to threaten Mitanni. Thutmose III fought 14 major campaigns in Palestine and Syria. Inscriptions in the temple of Karnak record booty won on these campaigns and a relief shows exotic plants, birds, and animals collected for the king in Syria.

Egypt and Mitanni eventually made peace. Thutmose IV and his son, Amonhotep III, both married princesses of Mitanni and sent gifts of gold in return. Under Akhenaten, however, foreign affairs were neglected and parts of the empire broke away from Egyptian control.

By the 19th Dynasty Mitanni had declined and Egypt's chief rival in the Near East was the Hittite empire. The Hittites, a warlike people whose

▲ The two-wheeled horse-drawn chariot was introduced into Egypt by the Hyksos people. The Egyptians soon learned to use chariots against their Near Eastern enemies.

▼ An 18th-Dynasty painting showing tribute bearers from Syria. The tribute includes fine gold vessels and a horn filled with perfumed oil. The child could be a slave or a hostage.

homeland was the mountains of Anatolia—now in modern Turkey, more than 600 miles (965 km) from Thebes—battled with Seti I and Ramesses II for control of Syria.

The battle of Qadesh saw the forces of Egypt under Ramesses II and the Hittites under Muwatallis fight for control of Syria (see page 41). It resulted in a victory for Ramesses II, but a few years later he signed a peace treaty with the Hittites and married a Hittite princess. The Hittite empire was destroyed in the 12th century B.C.E. by the mass migration of the Sea Peoples (see page 37). Egypt narrowly escaped being overwhelmed by the Sea Peoples, and all of its Near Eastern empire was lost.

▼ Egypt and the Near East (c.1530–1190 B.C.E.). Egypt traded with Cyprus, Crete, and Mycenaean Greece. The great Near Eastern powers were the Mitannis, Hittites, Babylonians, and Assyrians.

Northern frontiers of the Egyptian Empire

1 Farthest point reached by Thutmose I.

2 Frontier at the end of Thutmose III's reign.

3 Frontier in year 7 of Amonhotep II.

4 Frontier under Thutmose IV.

5 Frontier under Tutankhamon.

6 Frontier in year 21 of Ramesses II.

Hittite empire The pink area shows the Hittite empire at its greatest extent. The capital was Hattusas, in the north.
Assyria The Assyrians rose in power after the decline of Mitanni.

Boğazköy
(Hattusas)

HITTITE EMPIRE

ANATOLIA

GREECE (Mycenae)

(KIZZUWATNA)

Tell Fakariya (Washukanni)

(Carchemish)

MITANNI
(NAHARIN)

(Assur)

Crete
(Keftiu)   (Knossos)

CYPRUS
(ALASHIYA)

Ras Shamra
(Ugarit)   (Niya)

1
2

SYRIA

MESOPOTAMIA

ASSYRIA

Euphrates

Qadesh   3
4

(Byblos)   5

Damascus

Mediterranean Sea

Tigris

(Babylon)

BABYLON

(Megiddo)

PALESTINE

Gaza   (Lachish)

LIBYA

San el-Hagar (Tanis)
Tell Basta (Bubastis)

(Memphis)

Timna

el-Hiba
(Ankyronon Polis)

Serabit el-Khadim

el-Amarna
(Akhetaten)

Nile

Karnak (Ipet-Isut)
Luxor (Thebes)

*Red
Sea*

EGYPT   Aswan (Elephantine)
NUBIA

Aniba (Miam)

(Buhen)

Aniba   Modern name
(Miam)   Ancient name
⬜   Hittite empire c.1370–1330 B.C.E.
■   Capital city
●   Other site
?   Possible location

— 2 Northern frontier of the Egyptian empire

Scale 1: 13 000 000
0   400 km
0   300 miles

Gebel Barkal
(Napata)

On this clay tablet, dating to 1355 B.C.E., is a letter from King Tushratta of Mitanni to Amonhotep III of Egypt. It is part of an archive of correspondence found at el-Amarna. It is written in cuneiform with an Egyptian translation, in the hieratic script, at the bottom. The letter is about a statue of the goddess Ishtar sent to Egypt to help cure Amonhotep III. The king's complaint may have been toothache, since his mummy had terrible tooth decay.

The Egyptian Army

THE EGYPTIANS DO NOT SEEM TO HAVE been a particularly warlike people by nature. Egyptian accounts of the "ideal man" make little mention of qualities such as strength, courage, or skill in battle.

There was no large permanent army in the Old Kingdom. Troops were mustered as the need arose. They were led by officials rather than by professional soldiers. Such troops seem to have spent more time carrying out tasks such as quarrying minerals in the desert than fighting.

In the Middle Kingdom the army was larger, and fierce Nubian tribesmen were employed as mercenary soldiers. The great chain of fortresses built along the Nile to subdue Nubia needed permanent garrisons. At this period the army consisted of foot soldiers equipped with bows and arrows and copper-headed spears or axes. Other weapons used were copper daggers and wooden clubs and throwsticks. Large shields of stiffened cowhide were carried, but no helmets or body armor were worn.

By the time of the New Kingdom, Egypt had a large professional army that carried new or improved weapons. Stronger axheads and dagger blades were cast in bronze, and the scimitar—a fearsome curved sword—came into use. A new type of bow with greater range and power was also made.

Charioteers—the king's elite force

From the 18th Dynasty onwards the army was divided into infantry and chariotry. The horse-drawn chariots were made of wood and leather and were sometimes decorated with gold. They each carried two men: the charioteer who drove and the chariot warrior who was armed with a bow and a spear or sword. Such warriors might wear a protective tunic of leather or bronze.

In the early stages of a battle the chariot division would charge the enemy forces at great speed, with the chariot warriors firing off arrows. The chariotry was the elite of the Egyptian army and was often led by the king in person.

▼ Ramesses II's army in camp. Chariot horses are tethered in rows waiting to be fed and watered, while close by a chariot is being repaired. A company of foot soldiers is drilled by its standard-bearer, and the king's pet lion is being taken for a walk. None of the soldiers has a helmet; thick wigs or bushy hairstyles cushioned the head from the enemy's blows. The weapons shown include shields made of cowhide stretched on wooden frames and a bow made from two antelope horns lashed together.

Famous battles

Detailed accounts survive of some New Kingdom battles. The annals of Thutmose III at Karnak relate how the king led a surprise attack on the Palestinian city of Megiddo in 1456 B.C.E. He took his army on a risky shortcut through a narrow ravine. After a battle and a seven-month siege the city surrendered. Among the booty plundered were 924 chariots and more than 2,000 horses.

Even more is known about the battle fought between Ramesses II and the Hittite king Muwatallis in northern Syria in 1285 B.C.E. Misled by false information, the Egyptians were ambushed as they set up camp near the city of Qadesh. One division of the Egyptian army scattered in panic but Ramesses rallied his remaining troops and held off the enemy until reinforcements arrived. It is claimed in a poem that Ramesses fought this battle "like a fierce lion in a valley of goats." The king's courage turned a near disaster into an Egyptian victory. Losses were heavy on both sides.

These details from the Battle of Qadesh are based on reliefs in temples built by Ramesses II. Ramesses II's army had four main divisions named after Egyptian gods. The King was with Amon, the leading division, which set up camp near Qadesh, not knowing that the Hittite army was hidden behind the city. The Ra division was attacked by the Hittite chariotry. It broke and fled. The Hittites chased it to the Egyptian camp. Ramesses and his guard fought their way through the Hittite lines towards the approaching Ptah division. After a fierce battle, the Hittites retreated.

Egypt Divided

BY THE END OF THE 20TH DYNASTY EGYPT had lost Nubia as well as its Near Eastern empire. The late 20th-Dynasty kings in their Delta capital had little influence over Upper Egypt. The High Priest of Amon, controller of the vast wealth of the temple of Karnak, was the effective ruler of the south. The office of high priest was now always held by members of one family.

The Third Intermediate Period

On the death of the last 20th-Dynasty ruler, a king called Smendes claimed power in the north of the country. At the start of the era known as the Third Intermediate Period the capital was Tanis in the northeastern Delta. The 21st-Dynasty kings brought statues, obelisks, and decorated blocks from earlier reigns to adorn this city.

The dynasty of high priests situated at Thebes acknowledged the claims of the 21st-Dynasty kings, but continued to rule the south. Even in the Delta power was soon disputed.

Dynastic rivalries

During the late New Kingdom large numbers of Libyans had settled in Lower Egypt and become a force there. A family of Libyan descent provided the first king of the 22nd Dynasty, Shoshenq I. He was a vigorous ruler who recovered a number of Egypt's former territories in Palestine.

By this time the Jews had established the kingdom of Judah. Shoshenq attacked Judah and carried off a large quantity of treasure taken from the temple at Jerusalem. His campaigns are recorded in the buildings that he added to the temple of Karnak.

Shoshenq installed his own son as high priest at Thebes, so that all of Egypt was dominated by a single dynasty again. This fragile unity lasted only for about a century. Then there were rebellions in the south and a rival dynasty, the 23rd, was established in the Delta. Egypt began to split up into small areas whose rulers called themselves kings. Two of the most important of these kings were the rulers of Hermopolis and Herakleopolis.

King Osorkon IV of the 23rd Dynasty tried to control the south by abolishing the by-then hereditary office of high priest of Amon and by making his daughter high priestess instead. The high priestess was supposed to be the bride of the god Amon. This meant that she could not marry a human husband nor found a dynasty that would rival that of the royal family.

◀ The funeral mask of Psusennes I, recovered from his tomb at Tanis.

Osorkon III 883–855
Takelot II 860–835
Shoshenq III 835–783

23rd Dynasty c.828–712
Rulers of Thebes, Hermopolis, Herakleopolis, Leontopolis, and Tanis. The order of these kings is uncertain and some would have been contemporaries. They include:
Pedubaste I 828–803
Osorkon IV 777–749
Peftjauawybast 740–725

24th Dynasty 724–712
Rulers of Sais:
Tefnakhte 724–717
Bocchoris 717–712

25th Dynasty 770–712
Ruling Nubia and the Theban area:
Kashta 770–750
Piye 750–712
(*25th-Dynasty kings continued on page 44*)

Selected kings 5—
The Third Intermediate Period 1070–712 B.C.E.

21st Dynasty 1070–945
Smendes 1070–1044
Amenemnisu 1044–1040
Psusennes I 1040–992
Amenemope 993–984

Osorkon I 984–978
Siamun 978–959
Psusennes II 959–945

22nd Dynasty 945–712
Shoshenq I 945–924
Osorkon II 924–909
Takelot I 909–?
Shoshenq II ?–883

▲ A 22nd-Dynasty gold case containing a rolled strip of papyrus. The hieroglyphs are a promise from the god Khons to protect the wearer.

Kings out of Nubia

All of Nubia was now ruled by the kings of Napata (see page 45). Though Nubian by birth, they had adopted Egyptian culture and religion. They built pyramids and were devoted to the worship of Amon. One of these 25th-Dynasty rulers, Kashta, gained power over the region between Aswan and Thebes.

Kashta's successor, Piye, invaded Egypt, claiming that he was restoring order and the proper worship of the gods. Many Egyptian practices were adopted in Nubia during this period, including the building of pyramids as royal tombs. Piye forced the high priestess at Thebes to adopt his sister as her successor. He crushed the local ruler of Hermopolis and led his army and fleet as far north as Memphis. After a fierce battle, King Piye entered the city and gave thanks for his victory in the temple of Ptah. Tefnakhte, a chieftain who ruled the western Delta, was among the rulers who were forced to submit to Piye and send him treasure. After the Nubian king returned south, Tefnakhte continued to dominate the Delta. He was the first 24th-Dynasty ruler of Sais.

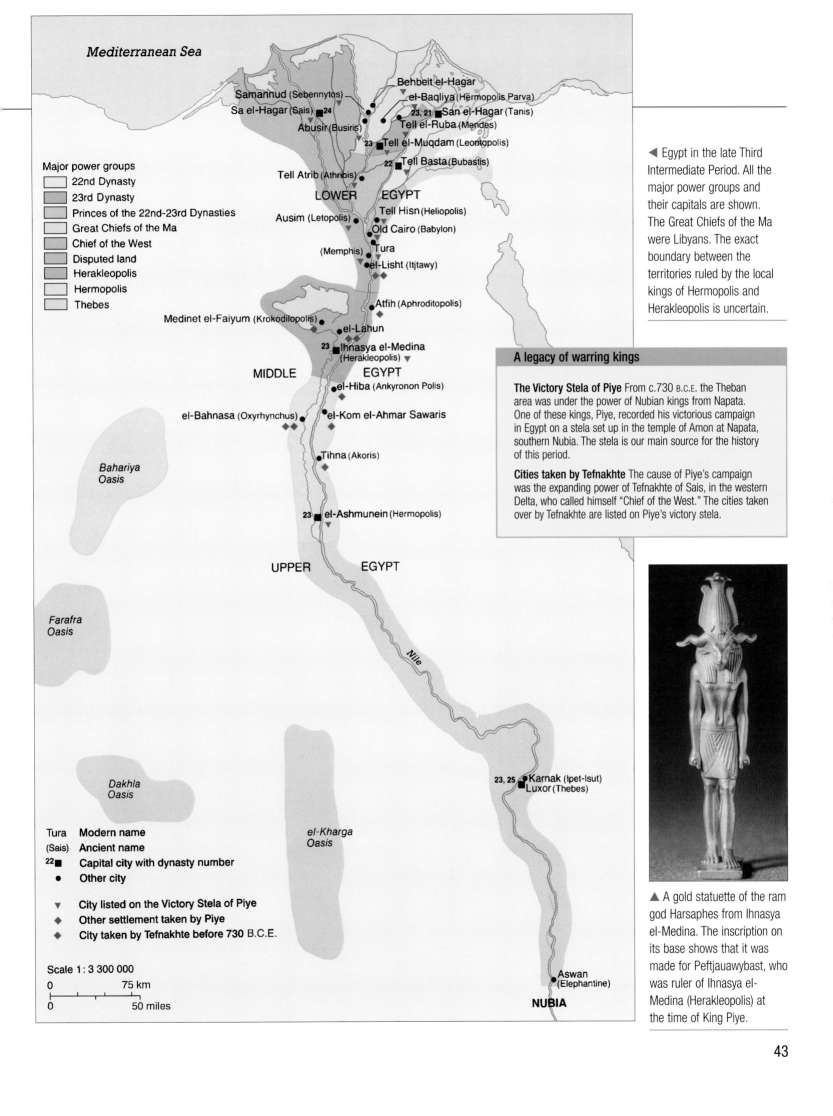

Mediterranean Sea

Major power groups
- 22nd Dynasty
- 23rd Dynasty
- Princes of the 22nd-23rd Dynasties
- Great Chiefs of the Ma
- Chief of the West
- Disputed land
- Herakleopolis
- Hermopolis
- Thebes

Behbeit el-Hagar
Samannud (Sebennytos)
el-Baqliya (Hermopolis Parva)
Sa el-Hagar (Sais) 24
23, 21 San el-Hagar (Tanis)
Abusir (Busiris)
Tell el-Ruba (Mendes)
23 Tell el-Muqdam (Leontopolis)
22 Tell Basta (Bubastis)
Tell Atrib (Athribis)

LOWER EGYPT

Tell Hisn (Heliopolis)
Ausim (Letopolis)
Old Cairo (Babylon)
(Memphis) Tura
el-Lisht (Itjtawy)

Atfih (Aphroditopolis)
Medinet el-Faiyum (Krokodilopolis)
el-Lahun
23 Ihnasya el-Medina
(Herakleopolis)

MIDDLE EGYPT

el-Hiba (Ankyronon Polis)
el-Bahnasa (Oxyrhynchus)
el-Kom el-Ahmar Sawaris

Tihna (Akoris)

Bahariya
Oasis

23 el-Ashmunein (Hermopolis)

UPPER EGYPT

Farafra
Oasis

Nile

Dakhla
Oasis

23, 25 Karnak (Ipet-Isut)
Luxor (Thebes)

el-Kharga
Oasis

Tura **Modern name**
(Sais) **Ancient name**
22■ **Capital city with dynasty number**
● **Other city**
▼ **City listed on the Victory Stela of Piye**
◆ **Other settlement taken by Piye**
◆ **City taken by Tefnakhte before 730 B.C.E.**

Scale 1 : 3 300 000
0   75 km
0   50 miles

Aswan
(Elephantine)
NUBIA

◄ Egypt in the late Third Intermediate Period. All the major power groups and their capitals are shown. The Great Chiefs of the Ma were Libyans. The exact boundary between the territories ruled by the local kings of Hermopolis and Herakleopolis is uncertain.

A legacy of warring kings

The Victory Stela of Piye From c.730 B.C.E. the Theban area was under the power of Nubian kings from Napata. One of these kings, Piye, recorded his victorious campaign in Egypt on a stela set up in the temple of Amon at Napata, southern Nubia. The stela is our main source for the history of this period.

Cities taken by Tefnakhte The cause of Piye's campaign was the expanding power of Tefnakhte of Sais, in the western Delta, who called himself "Chief of the West." The cities taken over by Tefnakhte are listed on Piye's victory stela.

▲ A gold statuette of the ram god Harsaphes from Ihnasya el-Medina. The inscription on its base shows that it was made for Peftjauawybast, who was ruler of Ihnasya el-Medina (Herakleopolis) at the time of King Piye.

The Last Egyptian Rulers

AFTER PIYE, THE NEXT 25TH-DYNASTY KING was Shabaka. He defeated a king claiming to rule the Delta from Sais and destroyed all other opposition. Shabaka then ruled a united kingdom of Egypt and Napata from Memphis. Egypt prospered at this time, but the whole of West Asia was entering a period of turmoil in which great empires rose and fell.

The Assyrian conquest of Egypt

In the seventh century B.C.E. the Assyrians were trying to extend their empire into Palestine. Egypt formed a defensive alliance with the kingdom of Judah. This angered the Assyrians. Their first attempt to invade Egypt was unsuccessful, but then in c.671 B.C.E., the Assyrian king Esarhaddon captured Memphis.

The 25th-Dynasty king Taharqa fled to Napata and Egypt was forced to pay tribute to the Assyrians. The local ruler of Sais, Necho, was allowed to call himself a king in return for serving the Assyrians. Necho was killed fighting Tantamani, the successor of Taharqa. The next Assyrian king, Assurbanipal, drove Tantamani back to Napata and sacked Thebes.

Necho's son, Psammetichus, was left as a puppet ruler in the Delta, but once trouble arose for the Assyrians in other parts of their empire he managed to drive them out and make himself king of all Egypt.

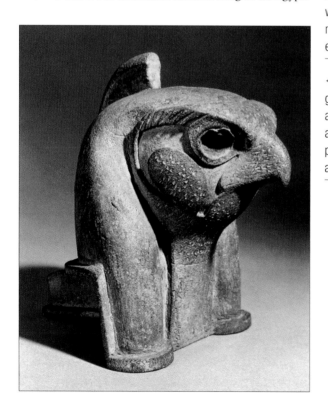

Selected kings 6—
The Late Period 712–332 B.C.E.

25th Dynasty 712–657
Ruling Egypt and Nubia:
Shabaka 712–698
Shebitku 698–690
Taharqa 690–664
Tantamani 664–657

26th Dynasty 664–525
Kings from Sais:
Necho I 672–664
Psammetichus I 664–610
Necho II 610–595
Psammetichus II 595–589
Apries 589–570
Amasis 570–526
Psammetichus III 526–525

27th Dynasty 525–404
(1st Persian period)
Cambyses 525–522
Darius 1 521–486
Xerxes I 486–466
Artaxerxes I 465–424
Darius II 424–404

28th Dynasty 404–399
Amyrtaios 404–399

29th Dynasty 399–380
Nepherites I 399–393
Hakoris 393–380

30th Dynasty 380–343
Nectanebo I 380–362
Teos 365–360
Nectanebo II 360–343

2nd Persian Period
Artaxerxes III 343–338
Arses 338–336
Darius III 335–332

Period interrupted by a native rule, Khababash

◄ This quartzite head is thought to be of King Amasis.

▶ An important priest shown as a scribe. In the Late Period artists often copied or adapted ideas from Old Kingdom art. This piece dates from about 650 B.C.E. but it was inspired by scribe statues made almost 2,000 years earlier (see page 32).

◄ Bronze head of a hawk god. This head was probably attached to a wooden staff and carried in temple processions. Fine bronzes are a feature of Late Period art.

Mediterranean Sea

Samannud (Sebennytos)
Sa el-Hagar
(Sais) 26, 28
(Naukratis)
Kom Abu Billo (Terenuthis)

Tell el-Ruba (Mendes)
• Gaza
•Jerusalem
(Jerusalem)
Dead
Sea
JUDAH
Tell el-Farama (Pelusium)
Tell el-Muqdam (Leontopolis)
Tell el-Yahudiya
(Leontopolis)
Saqqara •(Memphis)
25

A Abusir (Busiris)
B San el-Hagar (Tanis)
C Tell Atrib (Athribis)
D Saft el-Hinna
(Per-Sopdu)

LOWER EGYPT

Ihnasya el-Medina
(Herakleopolis)

Nile–Red Sea Canal

SINAI

MIDDLE   EGYPT

*Bahariya
Oasis*

*Farafra
Oasis*

el-Ashmunein (Hermopolis)

Asyut (Lykopolis)

Nile

*Dakhla
Oasis*

(Hibis)•

*el-Kharga
Oasis*

Girga (Thinis)

Red Sea

Karnak (Ipet-Isut)
Luxor (Thebes)

UPPER   EGYPT

EGYPT Aswan (Elephantine)

NUBIA

LOWER NUBIA

Karanog
Abu Simbel
Faras
(Buhen)
Semna

Wadi el-Arab

Firka

NAPATA-MEROE

Tabo

Kawa

Gebel Barkal
(Napata)
el-Kurru   Nuri

Debba

Kawa Modern name
(Sais) Ancient name
▨ Fertile land
• Stela of Darius
- - ➤ Route of Psammetichus' army

Egyptian sites
²⁸■ Capital city with dynasty number
▼ City in Assurbanipal's annals
• Other

Nubian sites
■ Capital city
◆ Napata-Meroe

Begrawiya
(Meroe)

Wad Ban Naqa

Scale 1 : 7 000 000
0   150 km
0   100 miles

Saba

Egypt allies with Greece

Under the Saite kings of the 26th Dynasty art
and literature flourished, but Egypt was rarely
at peace. Babylon became a greater power than
Assyria. In 601 B.C.E. Necho II repelled an invasion
by Nebuchadnezzar of Babylon. Psammetichus II
led an army deep into Nubia to intimidate the ruler
of Napata. The next king, Apries, was deposed by
Amasis, an Egyptian general. By this time many
Greeks were serving in the Egyptian army, and
Amasis encouraged the establishment of a Greek
trading settlement at Naukratis.

The Persian invasion

By the late sixth century B.C.E. Persia had become
the main power in West Asia. In 525 B.C.E.
the Persian ruler Cambyses invaded Egypt. He
successfully overthrew the Egyptian pharaoh,
Psammetichus III, to become the first ruler of the
27th Dynasty (first Persian period).

Cambyses shocked the ancient world by his
brutality and his contempt for local deities. His
successor, Darius I, was more humane, but the
Egyptians bitterly resented Persian rule. As a result,
there were rebellions led by a series of Egyptian
dynasties. None was successful for very long.

In the late fourth century B.C.E. the whole of the
Persian empire was conquered by the young king of
Macedon, Alexander the Great. After capturing
Persian naval bases farther north, he marched into
Egypt and was hailed as a savior by the Egyptians.

Invasion and conquest during the Late Period

The annals of Assurbanipal This Assyrian king left detailed records
of his wars. He lists cities in Egypt whose rulers paid homage to
him. These petty rulers are described as kings, showing how
divided Egypt had become.

The route of Psammetichus's army The route probably taken by
Psammetichus II when he invaded Napata in 591 B.C.E. Evidence
for the route comes from graffiti left by his army. Many of his
soldiers were Greek mercenaries.

Stelae of Darius The Persian king Darius I completed a canal begun
by Necho II. This canal linked a branch of the Nile River to the
Red Sea. Darius set up four stelae recording this achievement
along the banks of the canal.

◄ Egypt and the kingdom of Napata-Meroe, united under
Shabaka before the Assyrian conquest. Meroe became the
Nubian capital c.591 B.C.E. The kingdom of Meroe endured
until the fourth century C.E.

Greek and Roman Rule

WHEN ALEXANDER THE GREAT DIED IN 323 B.C.E. his empire began to break up. A Macedonian general, Ptolemy, brought Alexander's body to Egypt and built a tomb for him in the new city of Alexandria in the Delta. In 304 B.C.E. Ptolemy declared himself king of Egypt. He and his descendants ruled Egypt for more than 250 years.

Scholars and artists were encouraged to come to Alexandria, and Ptolemy established an extensive library there. Many Greeks and Macedonians were also given grants of land in Egypt. The officials appointed by the Ptolemies were almost always Greek rather than Egyptian.

A murderous family

Ptolemaic kings usually married their sisters. These royal ladies often acted as co-rulers. There were frequent power struggles within the family, and many Ptolemaic rulers seized or kept the throne by murdering close relations.

There were some rebellions against Greek rule in Upper Egypt. The Ptolemies tried to please their Egyptian subjects by building splendid temples to the Egyptian gods.

By the first century B.C.E. Rome had become the greatest power in the ancient world. The Romans wanted Egypt for its gold and its grain.

▲ A coin of Cleopatra VII. The Egyptians had no coins until Greek rule.

Queen Cleopatra VII

In 48 B.C.E. the great Roman general Julius Caesar intervened in an Egyptian civil war to support Cleopatra as ruler. The first Ptolemy to learn Egyptian, Cleopatra captivated Julius Caesar by her wit and beauty. A son was born to them.

After Julius Caesar was murdered another Roman general, Mark Antony, fell in love with Cleopatra. Antony and Cleopatra ruled the east together until they were attacked by Julius Caesar's heir, Octavian (Augustus). Antony and Cleopatra were defeated and forced to take their own lives. Egypt became just another province of the Roman Empire.

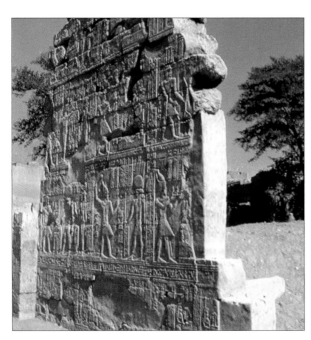

▲ Part of the ruined temple of the hawk god Montu at Tod, built under Ptolemy VIII. In such temples Ptolemaic rulers are shown in Egyptian royal dress carrying out the rituals of Egyptian religion.

◄ Terra-cotta figurine of the Egyptian dwarf god Bes, from Roman Egypt. Bes, the protector of children and pregnant women, was one of the Egyptian deities who became popular with Greek and Roman settlers in Egypt. He holds a Roman shield.

► A second-century C.E. coffin decorated with Egyptian religious scenes and a portrait of the deceased.

Mediterranean Sea

Mersa Matruh (Paraetonium)
Rosetta
Gaza
Alexandria (Alexandria)
Tell el-Timai (Thmuis)
Tell el-Farama (Pelusium)
(Naukratis)
LOWER   EGYPT
Kom Abu Billo (Terenuthis)
Tell Atrib (Athribis)
Trajan's Canal
Saqqara (Memphis)
FAIYUM
SINAI
(Arsinoe)
Ihnasya el-Medina (Herakleopolis)
Siwa Oasis
el-Bahnasa (Oxyrhynchus)
Bahariya Oasis
Via Hadriana
Eastern Desert
el-Ashmunein (Hermopolis)
el-Sheikh Ibada (Antinoopolis)
Tuna el-Gebel (Hermopolis)
UPPER   EGYPT
(Myos Hormos)
Farafra Oasis
(Mons Porphyrites) PORPHYRY
Red Sea
(Mons Claudianus) GRANITE
(Aphrodito)
Western Desert
Akhmim (Panopolis)
(Philoteras)
Qena (Kaine)
GOLD
Quseir (Leukos Limen)
Dakhla Oasis
Dendara (Iunet)
Qift (Koptos)
Wadi Hammamat
Laqeita (Phoinikon)
Tod
(Hibis)
Luxor (Thebes)
Gebelein (Per-Hathor)
Esna (Latopolis)
Tod   Modern name
(Talmis) Ancient name
Edfu (Apollinopolis Magna)
el-Kharga Oasis
(Mons Smaragdus) EMERALDS
Fertile land
GRANITE Resource
Site of resource
Kom Ombo (Ombos)
Roman way-station
Roman road
EGYPT (Philae)
Aswan (Elephantine)
Desert route
NUBIA   Dabod
LOWER NUBIA (DODEKASCHOINUS)
(Berenike)
Capital city
Settlement or site
Kalabsha (Talmis)
Types of site
Dendur (Tutzis)
Papyrus
el-Dakka (Pselchis)
Other

Scale 1 : 5 000 000
0   100 km
0   75 miles

Desert finds and Roman roads

Papyrus sites Sites at which papyri or ostraca written on in ancient Greek were found. They include plays and poems, books on medicine and mathematics, and numerous personal letters. Many great works of Greek and Roman literature survive only in copies that were preserved in the hot dry sand of Egypt. Papyrus production was a major industry in Alexandria.

Roman way-stations The Romans built a road network in the Eastern Desert. Way-stations were provided with water supplies to make it easier for expeditions to cross the desert. The Romans quarried granite and porphyry, a stone used for statues and vessels, and mined for emeralds. The roads led to ports on the Red Sea. The Persian-built canal linking the Nile River to the Red Sea was improved under the emperor Trajan.

▲ Egypt in the Greco-Roman Period. In the Ptolemaic era most of the country's wealth was centered on Alexandria, the capital. Land reclamation schemes and improved irrigation made the Faiyum into a prosperous agricultural area. Many Greeks settled there. Group tombs full of gilded mummies have been found at Bahariya Oasis.

Roman rule

Roman Egypt was ruled by prefects who were appointed by the emperor. Temples continued to be built to the Egyptian gods, and the worship of Isis spread throughout the empire. Greek and Roman settlers also adopted some Egyptian burial customs.

The native Egyptians were given very little power in their own country. They lived under Roman law, and heavy taxation meant that most Egyptian people were forced to live in extreme poverty. Egyptian culture was finally destroyed when Christianity became the official religion of the Roman Empire in the fourth century C.E.

Women of Egypt

WOMEN WERE TREATED BETTER IN ancient Egypt than they have been in many other societies. Egyptian women could own and manage property. They had many legal rights and were permitted to speak for themselves in court. A woman did not lose control of her own property when she married. If there was a divorce, the wife could claim part of her husband's assets to support herself and her children.

Very few women were taught to read and write, however. This barred them from most careers in government service. Women did serve in temples as part-time priestesses.

Royal women

The women of the royal family were usually priestesses. They played the roles of goddesses in some royal rituals. The mother of the reigning king was an important figure.

Royal women could act as regents. Queen Ahhotep, for example, ruled on behalf of her young son Ahmose and even led troops into battle. The Great Royal Wife could also be a power in the land. Queen Tiye, the consort of Amonhotep III, was a commoner by birth, but foreign kings wrote humble letters to her and she was worshiped as a goddess in her own lifetime.

The throne sometimes passed through the female line, and a few women ruled in their own right. Queens such as Hatshepsut and Cleopatra VII are among Egypt's most outstanding rulers.

▶ A colossal statue of Merytamun, a daughter of Ramesses II, recently found at Akhmim. Like some other princesses, Merytamun acted as an official consort for her father. She is seen wearing an elaborate crown topped by a pair of feathers.

▼ A group of female entertainers in a banquet scene from an 18th-Dynasty Theban tomb. One woman plays a double flute and another claps out the rhythm while two girls dance naked. The women wear cones of scented fat on top of their wigs. Music, singing, and dancing were among the few professions that were open to women, but such entertainers probably had a low status in society.

▶ The dwarf Seneb embraced by his wife. In front are their young son and daughter. This Sixth-Dynasty family group comes from Seneb's tomb at Giza. Later statues often show husbands and wives with their arms around each other.

Family life

The majority of women spent their lives running a household and raising a family. In Egyptian society men were allowed to have more than one wife at a time, but very few did.

Egyptian "Wisdom Books," which tell young men how to behave, advise getting married as early as possible. They also warn husbands not to order their wives around at home. Women were thought to be competent enough to run the home without interference from men.

The importance of family life is stressed in Egyptian art. Men are regularly shown beside their wives and mothers. Sons and daughters appear making offerings to their parents. Couples hoped for large families but many Egyptian women died during childbirth while still young.

▶ In this Old Kingdom bedroom scene an important official called Mereruka relaxes while his wife plays the harp. In Egyptian art women are nearly always young, slender, and beautiful. Men have skin darkened to reddish brown by exposure to the sun. Women are given pale yellow skin, suggesting that their place was indoors.

Part Two

A Journey Down the Nile

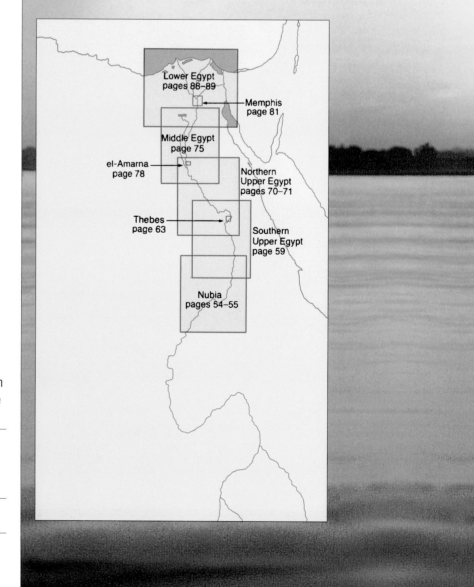

▲ A sphinx from the temple of Ramesses II at el-Sebua, which was flooded by the construction of the Aswan High Dam in the 1960s.

▶ Boats sailing on the Nile. At 4,185 mi (6,730 km) from its source in Uganda to the tip of the Delta, it is the world's longest river.

Inset: Key to maps in this section of the book.

Boats on the Nile

BOATS WERE THE MOST IMPORTANT FORM of transportation in ancient Egypt. The earliest boats were small skiffs made from bundles of papyrus stalks lashed together with ropes. The skiffs were propelled by paddles or long poles. Papyrus skiffs were used throughout Egyptian history for hunting or fishing in the marshes.

At least as early as the Old Kingdom large boats were built of wood. Because of the shortage of tall trees, these boats had to be made from numerous small pieces of wood. For seagoing craft and the biggest Nile boats, planks of cedar were imported from Lebanon.

In the New Kingdom warships and trading vessels were built in a great dockyard at Memphis. Ships were given names like *The King is Mighty*, *Splendor of the Sun Disk*, and *Star in Memphis*.

Sailing the Nile

For most of its course in Upper Egypt the Nile was a broad and placid river. Many branches of the Nile in the Delta were also navigable by large boats. The wind was usually from the north, so sail was used for upstream (southward) journeys. For traveling downstream (north) oars were needed.

The Egyptians rarely sailed at night. Shifting sandbanks were a major hazard to ships. During the day sailors kept watch for them from lookout posts. To avoid getting stuck on sandbanks, most of the hull of a Nile-going boat had to lie above the waterline. The boats also needed to be light, particularly because south of Aswan vessels had to be dragged ashore and hauled past the dangerous Cataracts (see map on pages 10–11).

Boats and cargoes

Boats were used for transporting all kinds of cargo from obelisks to cattle. Most Egyptian boats had no keels, so their shallow hulls were not very strong. Cargo was usually carried on deck and cabins were also above deck.

The heaviest cargoes, such as blocks of Aswan granite, were loaded onto long narrow barges that were towed by other vessels. Most moving of stone was done when the river was at its highest, just after the inundation (flood).

Few Egyptians could swim and crocodiles made the water dangerous, so ferries were used for crossing the river. The wealthy had pleasure craft. One story tells that when King Snofru was hot and bored he would demand to be taken for a boat trip.

The world's oldest boats

The Egyptians imagined the sun god sailing across the sky in a boat. This may be why full-size boats were included in some royal burials from the Early Dynastic Period through the Middle Kingdom. A dismantled boat found in a pit beside the pyramid of Khufu at Giza has been reconstructed and is now in a special museum. The 140-foot (43-m) vessel is made up of 1,224 pieces of cedar. It dates to about 2528 B.C.E.

In the Middle and New Kingdoms model boats were sometimes placed in tombs. Their magical purpose was to help the tomb owner make a pilgrimage to Abydos, the city of Osiris, ruler of the dead. Sacred barks (boats) carried cult statues of gods. On land these statues were often carried in miniature barks by priests.

◀ ▶ Nile boats of different dates:
1 Predynastic Made from papyrus. It has a tall prow and stern and one large steering oar. **2 Old Kingdom** Wooden boat with typical Egyptian hull shape. It has steering gear and a double-footed mast. The sail is taller than it is wide. **3 Middle Kingdom** The steering gear is more elaborate and the mast is collapsible. There is one bank of oars on each side. **4 Late Period** A boat with a high stern and simple steering gear.

2

3

4

◀ A New Kingdom Nile-going vessel. This picture is based on a model boat from the tomb of Tutankhamon. The standard sail is now wider than it is tall. The deckhouse, or cabin, is in the center. A helmsman stands in front of a rudder post to control the steering oars by moving the tiller. There are lookout posts fore and aft. Royal vessels like this one were often beautifully decorated.

Lower Nubia

IN MOST OF ANCIENT NUBIA THE NILE VALLEY was very narrow. Some Nubian groups settled in the few areas of land that were suitable for agriculture. Others lived as nomads in the deserts. In the Old Kingdom the Egyptians often raided Lower Nubia to capture people and cattle. They also wanted to control the trade routes into Africa and the gold mines of the Nubian desert.

In the Middle Kingdom Egypt conquered all of Lower Nubia (see map opposite) and part of Upper Nubia (in present-day Sudan). A series of forts was built along the Nile River, mainly in the area of the Second and Third Cataracts. Egypt later lost control of Nubia, although some Egyptian people continued to live there.

Nubia was reconquered by Egypt in the New Kingdom. Towns and temples were built instead of forts. Perhaps as a result of years of drought, the population of Lower Nubia was very small by the end of the New Kingdom.

From the Late Period a native dynasty ruled the whole of Nubia. At their capitals of Napata and later Meroe they continued to build temples and pyramids in the Egyptian style for hundreds of years. A few temples to Egyptian and Nubian gods were built in Lower Nubia during the Greco-Roman Period. One Nubian tribe, the Blemmyes, worshiped the goddess Isis long after Egypt had become Christian.

Flooding of Nubia in modern times

The building of the new Aswan "High" Dam across the Nile River in the 1960s meant that much of Lower Nubia was flooded to create a giant reservoir known as Lake Nasser. But the United Nations had by then organized a huge campaign, funded by international donations, to dig and record all the main archaeological sites. Many exciting finds were made by archaeologists from all over the world. A great deal was learned about life in ancient Nubia.

The important monuments were moved to safety. Some temples, such as Abu Simbel and Amada, were dismantled and rebuilt on higher ground in the same area. Others, such as Kalabsha, were rebuilt at new sites. A few were re-erected outside Egypt. The temple of Dabod, for example, now stands in a park in Madrid, Spain. A wing was added to the Metropolitan Museum of Art in New York to house the temple of Dendur.

◄ A painting of the temple at Old Kalabsha as it looked in 1839. This was the largest free-standing temple in Lower Nubia. In 1962–63 it was dismantled and some 13,000 blocks of stone were moved to New Kalabsha close to the Aswan High Dam, where the temple was rebuilt.

Faras
Aksha
Serra East
Dibeira East
Dibeira West

Nile

Buhen
Kor • *Second Cataract*
Mirgissa (Iqen) •
Wadi Halfa

SOUTHERN
UPPER EGYPT
SEE PAGE 59

4

Nile

First Cataract □ Aswan

Aswan Dam

Aswan High Dam ● New Kalabsha
(Sadd el-Ali)
Dabod ▼

3

Tafa (Taphis) ●
▼
Beit el-Wali ● ● Old Kalabsha (Talmis)
▼

Dendur (Tutzis) ●
▼
Lake Nasser

Gerf Hussein ●
LOWER NUBIA ▼

el-Dakka (Pselchis) ● ● Quban (Contra Pselchis)
▼

Nile

Wadi Allaqi

New el-Sebua ● ● Old el-Sebua
▼ ▼

el-Derr ● ● Amada
Aniba (Miam) ▼ ▼
■ ● el-Lessiya
▼
Qasr Ibrim (Primis) ▼

NUBIA

▲ Major town
● Other modern town
• Location of ancient site
━━ International boundary
– – Regional boundary
━━ Road
〰 Course of ancient river

Abu Simbel ●
Abahuda ●
▼

Types of ancient site
● Settlement
▼ Temple
■ Tomb

Kor   Modern name
(Miam)   Ancient name

Scale 1:1 000 000
0   30 km
0   20 miles

2

1

A   B   C

Nubia • Sites

Abu Simbel

RAMESSES II BUILT SEVEN MAJOR TEMPLES in Nubia. The most famous of these are the two temples at Abu Simbel, known as the Great Temple and the Small Temple. They are built into a sandstone cliff.

Inside are two pillared halls decorated with rock-cut reliefs. Some show the pharaoh in his chariot fighting the Hittites at Qadesh. The boastful Ramesses was very proud of his role in this battle (see page 64).

The Great Temple was designed so that twice a year the rising sun would reach the innermost part and light up the statues of the gods. In the beautiful Small Temple, the Great Royal Wife Nefertari is shown being crowned as a goddess.

The rescue of the temples

In the 1960s the temples of Abu Simbel were in danger of disappearing beneath Lake Nasser. People from all over the world raised the sum of 40 million dollars to save them. The Great Temple was cut into 807 large blocks and the Small Temple into 235 blocks. An artificial cliff was built 215 feet (66 m) above the original site. The blocks were moved to the new site, put back together again, and covered by a vast concrete dome. The work took four and a half years. Now Abu Simbel is a wonder of modern technology, as well as a marvel of the ancient world.

1 Terrace
2 Grand entrance with colossi
3 Great pillared hall
4 Side rooms
5 Small pillared hall
6 Anteroom
7 Sanctuary with niche for cult statues

◀ A cutaway view showing the plan of the Great Temple. Most Egyptian temples had a walled forecourt, a grand entrance, one or more pillared (hypostyle) halls, and a sanctuary that housed the cult statues.

▲ A festival of the sun god at the Great Temple of Abu Simbel. The most important festivals were on the two days of the year when the sun's rays shone through the entrance and along the main axis to reach the sanctuary. Here, priests and a high official arrive by boat for the festival. In ancient times statues and reliefs were often brightly painted. The temples would have looked much more colorful than they do today. The rock-cut facade of the Great Temple has four 70-ft-(21-m-) high statues (colossi) of Ramesses II. His mother, his chief wife, and eight of his 140 children are shown on a much smaller scale at the feet of the statues.

Southern Upper Egypt

IN ANCIENT TIMES THE FRONTIER BETWEEN Egypt and Nubia was at Biga (see page 60). This island was submerged after the building of the Aswan High Dam. In the first four nomes of Upper Egypt (see map on page 14), the Nile valley is narrow and the desert is always close.

There was not much good agricultural land, but the deserts themselves were rich in minerals. Sandstone, granite, diorite, quartzite, and steatite (used for buildings and statues) were quarried close to Aswan. An amethyst mine was also situated in this area. Gold was mined in both the Eastern and the Nubian Deserts.

A temple from earliest times

The arid climate of Southern Upper Egypt is ideal for preserving ancient remains. We know more about the south of the country than we do about the marshy lands of northern Egypt, where excavation is difficult.

The first four nomes of Upper Egypt were important in Predynastic times. Hierakonpolis (modern name Kom el-Ahmar) was one of the earliest towns to be built in Egypt. The Predynastic settlement was a vibrant city extending more than 3 miles (5 km) along the edge of the Western Desert.

In the First Dynasty a new town and a temple were built on the floodplain. This is the oldest Egyptian temple that we know about in detail. Treasures found in it include mace heads and palettes that are the only record of some early Egyptian rulers. There were also ivory figurines, a golden hawk's head, and life-size copper statues of two Sixth-Dynasty kings.

An ancient town

Another site that was important from Predynastic times was Nekheb (modern el-Kab). This settlement developed into a typical Egyptian town. The houses were packed together inside a huge mud-brick enclosure wall. The main temple, dedicated to the local vulture goddess, was inside the town. It was rebuilt many times over a period of nearly 3,000 years. Smaller temples were built on the edge of the desert and the tombs of important people were cut into the desert cliffs.

In all main towns in ancient Egypt there was a necropolis. This was a "city" of the dead, in which the streets were lined with tombs instead of houses. The desert necropolises have often survived long after their corresponding towns on the floodplain have disappeared.

Temples of the Greco-Roman Period

The most remarkable survival in Southern Upper Egypt is the series of impressive temples dating to Greco-Roman times. There are examples at Philae, Aswan, Kom Ombo, Edfu, el-Kab, Esna, and Tod. Although they were built when the country was under foreign rule, they are Egyptian in style.

Edfu is the most famous and probably the best preserved, but the temples at Esna and Kom Ombo are also outstanding. Esna was dedicated to the ram god Khnum. A calendar inscribed on the walls tells us about the many festivals celebrated here. The temple at Kom Ombo is unusual because the left side is dedicated to one deity (the falcon god Haroeris, also known as Horus the Elder), and the right side to another deity—the crocodile god Sobek.

▼ Part of the Greco-Roman temple overlooking the Nile River at Kom Ombo. The chief deities here were Sobek, the crocodile god, and Haroeris— a form of Horus. Sacred crocodiles were reared in a pool in the temple grounds. Nearby was a cemetery for mummified crocodiles.

NORTHERN UPPER EGYPT
SEE PAGES 70–71

Eastern Desert

(Abydos) •

Qena (Kaine)

Hiw
(Diospolis Parva)

Qift (Koptos)

Valley of the Kings •

Luxor
(Thebes)

Armant (Hermonthis)

SEE PAGE 63
FOR MORE DETAIL

el-Rizeiqat

Tod

Western Desert

Gebelein (Per-Hathor)

el-Moalla

Esna (Latopolis)

Esna Barrage

el-Hella (Contra-Lato)

SOUTHERN

Kom Mer

Nile

el-Kula

el-Kab (Nekheb)

UPPER

Kom el-Ahmar
(Hierakonpolis)

Edfu
(Apollinopolis Magna)

EGYPT

Gebel el-Silsila

Kom Ombo (Ombos)

Major town

Other modern town

Location of ancient site

Regional boundary

Road

Ancient course of river

Fertile land

Types of ancient site

▲ Pyramid

Settlement

▼ Temple

■ Tomb

◆ Other

Tod   Modern name
(Philae)   Ancient name

Scale 1 : 1 000 000

0   30 km
0   20 miles

Aswan (Elephantine)

Ist Cataract
Aswan Dam
(Biga)

(Philae)

Aswan High Dam

NUBIA

SEE PAGES 54–55

Lake
Nasser

A

B

C

4

3

2

1

Southern Upper Egypt • Sites

City of Aswan

ASWAN TOOK ITS ANCIENT NAME OF Elephantine from the elephant-ivory trade. The main part of the city was situated on Elephantine Island in the middle of the Nile River. On the east bank of the river were stone quarries and a trading area. Tombs were cut in the cliffs of the west bank.

Aswan was close to the border between Egypt and Nubia. Troops were stationed there to protect the border and to take part in mining and trading expeditions. All the gold from the Nubian mines passed through Aswan. Donkey trains took desert routes from here to trade with African peoples.

In a Sixth-Dynasty tomb at Aswan there is an account of some of these trading trips. The tomb owner was a man named Harkhuf, who ended his days as a courtier. He tells how his explorations took him south three times. Each trip took seven or eight months. On the third trip he returned home with 300 donkeys carrying precious goods such as ivory, ebony, incense, and leopard skins.

Best of all, he had brought back a pygmy to dance for the king. Harkhuf proudly quotes a letter from King Pepy II. The king, who was only a young boy at the time, was thrilled to hear about the pygmy. He ordered Harkhuf to hurry immediately to the palace by boat. The pygmy was to be guarded day and night. "Check on him 10 times a night!" wrote Pepy. "My Majesty wants to see this pygmy more than all the treasures of Sinai and Punt!"

▼ An unfinished royal statue in the granite quarries east of Aswan. Stone quarried here was used in buildings all over ancient Egypt.

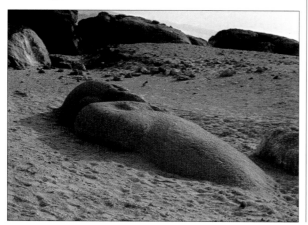

Holy islands—Philae & Biga

PHILAE AND BIGA ARE A PAIR OF ISLANDS in the Nile River just below Aswan. On Biga Island was the Abaton, a mound that was linked with the god Osiris.

When Set murdered Osiris he tore the body into many pieces. Biga was said to be the place where the left leg of Osiris was buried. In one version of the myth Isis, the wife of Osiris, collected the pieces and joined them by magic. Several places claimed to be the site where the whole body of Osiris was buried. Biga was one. The soul of Osiris was thought to haunt the island in the form of a bird. Biga was so holy that only priests could land there.

Philae was sacred to Isis. The temple of Isis was the largest of several temples and shrines on the island. Most of the buildings date to Greco-Roman times. Pilgrims came from all over the Roman Empire to worship Isis here.

The last known inscriptions in ancient Egyptian are at Philae. The religion of Egypt survived on this island for longer than in any other place.

Many of the buildings were still in excellent condition until construction of the first Aswan Dam began in 1898. Once the dam was finished, Philae and Biga were flooded for most of each year. When the second Aswan Dam was constructed they were permanently submerged. The temples of Philae were reassembled on Agilika Island about 600 yards (550 m) from their original home and are now well above the water level again.

▼ A Roman shrine on Philae island before it was moved to a new site. The discolored stone shows the level reached by the flood waters each year. In the foreground are the remains of the foundations of a small chapel.

Temple at Edfu

THERE WAS A WALLED TOWN AT EDFU FROM the Old Kingdom onwards. The site is now famous for its Temple of Horus. Few buildings from the ancient world are as well preserved as this temple. It was almost completely intact when it was first excavated in the 1860s. Inscriptions give many construction details. It was begun under Ptolemy III in 237 B.C.E. and took about 180 years to complete.

On the great pylon (gateway) Ptolemy XII strikes a group of prisoners with a mace. Egyptian kings had been shown in this pose for nearly 3,000 years. Inside the temple are reliefs depicting Horus fighting the enemies of his father, Osiris. The evil god Set turns himself into a hippopotamus, but Horus fearlessly hunts him down with a magical harpoon. This story was acted out each year during the festival of The Victory of Horus.

◄ The massive pillars of the hypostyle (Greek for "bearing pillars") hall at Edfu. The hall imitates a thicket of marsh plants. On some pillars the figures of the gods were damaged by early Christians and have been almost erased.

▼ The modern town of Edfu is dominated by the great temple dedicated to the god Horus. Its wonderful state of preservation is clear from this aerial view. The mound beyond the temple is the site of the ancient town.

The Great City of Thebes

IN THE TIME OF THE OLD KINGDOM, THEBES was no more than a provincial town. When a local dynasty reunited Egypt following the First Intermediate Period, Thebes became an important administrative and religious center. From the New Kingdom onwards it was one of the largest urban areas in the whole of Egypt. Its magnificent buildings were famous throughout the ancient world. Thebes is a Greek name. The Egyptians called the city Waset.

The total area of Thebes was about 3 square miles (8 sq. km). The city spread out on both sides of the Nile River. The east bank was reserved for the living, while the west bank was mainly for the dead. Today the site of Eastern Thebes is largely covered by the modern town of Luxor. Little remains of the ancient houses and palaces that once stood there, but some of the great stone temples survive.

The city of the dead

Western Thebes was dominated by the mountain known as "The Peak." The Egyptians believed that this mountain was an entrance to the underworld. Many tombs were cut into the cliffs and ravines close to the Peak. This necropolis (city of the dead) was called "The Place of Truth."

The artists and sculptors who decorated the royal tombs lived at Deir el-Medina in housing provided by the government. Their homes, shrines, and family tombs are so well preserved that we know more about these people than about any other ancient Egyptian community.

The Valley of the Kings

The pyramid burials of Old and Middle Kingdom rulers were soon robbed of their treasures. From the 18th Dynasty a new plan was tried. Enene, the chief architect of Amonhotep I and Thutmose I, tells us: "I oversaw the cutting out of the rock tomb of his Majesty in a lonely place where nobody could look on." This lonely place was the Valley of the Kings.

Throughout the New Kingdom rulers were buried in tombs that were hidden in this valley. Mortuary temples were built on the west bank to serve the cult of the dead kings. Some rulers also built palaces in Western Thebes. The largest was the palace of Amonhotep III at Malqata.

▼ A painted burial chamber in the Theban necropolis. This is the tomb of Pashed. He was one of the artists who worked on the royal tombs. The entrance to the burial chamber is flanked by the jackal god Anubis, who guarded the dead. On the rear wall are the gods who judged the dead.

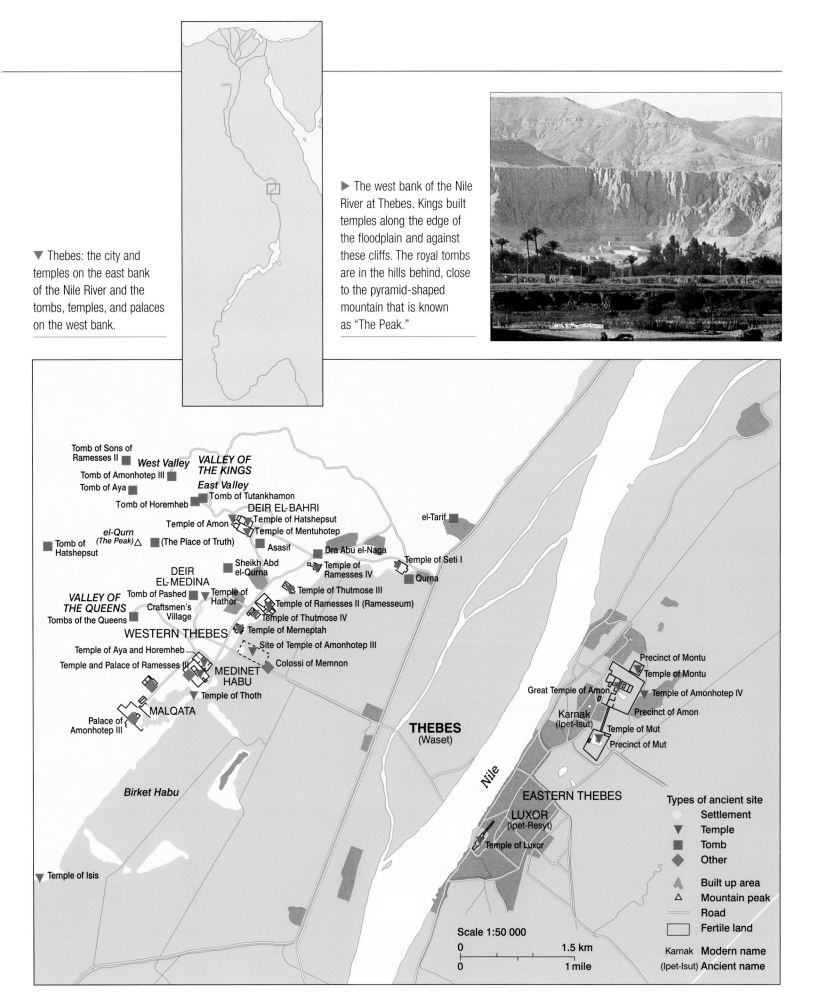

▼ Thebes: the city and temples on the east bank of the Nile River and the tombs, temples, and palaces on the west bank.

▶ The west bank of the Nile River at Thebes. Kings built temples along the edge of the floodplain and against these cliffs. The royal tombs are in the hills behind, close to the pyramid-shaped mountain that is known as "The Peak."

Tomb of Sons of Ramesses II
West Valley
VALLEY OF THE KINGS
Tomb of Amonhotep III
East Valley
Tomb of Aya
Tomb of Tutankhamon
Tomb of Horemheb
DEIR EL-BAHRI
Temple of Amon
Temple of Hatshepsut
Temple of Mentuhotep
el-Tarif
el-Qurn
(The Peak)△
(The Place of Truth)
Asasif
Dra Abu el-Naga
Temple of Seti I
Tomb of Hatshepsut
Sheikh Abd el-Qurna
Temple of Ramesses IV
Qurna
DEIR EL-MEDINA
Temple of Thutmose III
Tomb of Pashed
Temple of Hathor
Temple of Ramesses II (Ramesseum)
VALLEY OF THE QUEENS
Craftsmen's Village
Temple of Thutmose IV
Tombs of the Queens
Temple of Merneptah
WESTERN THEBES
Site of Temple of Amonhotep III
Temple of Aya and Horemheb
Colossi of Memnon
Temple and Palace of Ramesses III
MEDINET HABU
MALQATA
Temple of Thoth
Palace of Amonhotep III

Birket Habu

THEBES
(Waset)

Precinct of Montu
Temple of Montu
Great Temple of Amon
Temple of Amonhotep IV
Karnak
(Ipet-Isut)
Precinct of Amon
Temple of Mut
Precinct of Mut

EASTERN THEBES

Nile

LUXOR
(Ipet-Resyt)
Temple of Luxor

Temple of Isis

Types of ancient site
● Settlement
▼ Temple
■ Tomb
◆ Other
▲ Built up area
△ Mountain peak
— Road
▢ Fertile land
Karnak Modern name
(Ipet-Isut) Ancient name

Scale 1:50 000
0   1.5 km
0   1 mile

Pylon, pillars, and obelisks at Luxor

THE GOD AMON HAD TWO MAIN TEMPLES in Thebes: Karnak in the north of the city and Luxor in the south. Most of the Luxor temple was built in the 18th Dynasty during the reign of Amonhotep III. A courtyard and pylon (gateway) were added later by Ramesses II. An avenue of sphinxes joining Luxor to Karnak was set up during the Late Period.

Luxor has one of the most impressive entrances of any Egyptian temple. The pylon is decorated with the favorite subject of Ramesses II: his own bravery at the battle of Qadesh (see page 56). Outside the pylon are several colossal statues of this pharaoh. A pair of red granite obelisks once stood here, but one of them was taken to Paris in 1833.

The Festival of Opet

The temple has two courtyards. They are linked by a narrow colonnade, which formed a route for processions. The walls of this processional way are decorated with scenes from the Festival of Opet (also called the Beautiful Feast of Opet), which was one of the most important festivals that took place around Thebes. At this annual festival the Amon of Karnak visited Luxor for 11 days.

The cult statues of Amon, his wife Mut, and their son Khons were placed in magnificently decorated barks (boats). Huge crowds gathered on the east bank of the Nile to watch the barks towed from Karnak to Luxor. On shore the procession included musicians, dancers, and acrobats. Questions might be put to the god at this time. Occasionally the heir to the throne seems to have been chosen by Amon during the Festival of Opet.

Deep inside the temple is a room decorated with reliefs. They tell the story of the birth of Amonhotep III. They also show Amon taking the form of King Thutmose IV to visit Queen Mutemwiya. Many goddesses come also to nurse and protect the queen's son. The young prince is then brought before his father Amon and the gods decide to give him a long reign.

Close to this room is an area of the temple that was turned into a shrine to the Roman emperors around 300 C.E. Nearly 1,000 years later a mosque (Muslim place of worship) was built in the courtyard of Ramesses II. The mosque is still in use.

▶ A view of Luxor from the southwest. The mosque built into the temple is on the right.

▼ The pylon and courtyard built by Ramesses II. Behind are the tall columns of the processional way.

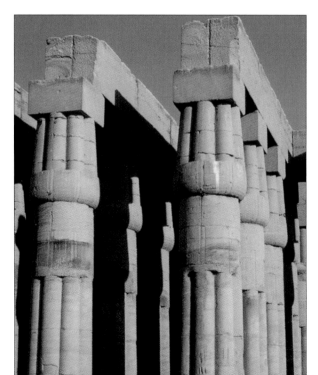

◀ Columns from the part of Luxor temple built by Amonhotep III. These columns imitate bundles of papyrus. Most Egyptian columns are based on plant forms.

Temple complex at Karnak

K ARNAK IS THE SITE OF A GROUP OF
temples covering an area of about 1 square
mile (2.6 sq. km). The most important was
the Great Temple of Amon. The name Amon means
"the hidden one," and he was the god of invisible
forces such as the wind. He was not an important
deity, however, until the Middle Kingdom. Very little
of the Middle Kingdom temple survives. Every
Egyptian ruler wanted to please Amon by putting
up splendid buildings for him at Karnak. This often
meant knocking down the old buildings and reusing
their stones. The Great Temple was continually
enlarged and rebuilt over a period of 2,000 years.

The Triumph of Amon

In the early 18th Dynasty Thebes became the capital
of Egypt. Amon's name was linked with that of the
sun god Ra. This new deity Amon-Ra was credited
with the creation of the world.

During the New Kingdom Karnak became the
largest and wealthiest temple complex in Egypt. The
Great Temple of Amon was once surrounded by tall
mud-brick walls. This enclosed area includes a sacred
lake and many lesser temples and shrines. The
eastern part of the Great Temple complex is the
oldest. Kings kept on building new entrances, so the
temple now has 10 massive pylons (gateways).

Between the second and third pylons is the Great
Hypostyle Hall, the most famous part of the temple.
The hall was begun by Seti I and finished by
Ramesses II. The roof of this vast hall is supported
by 134 elaborate columns. The 12 columns in the
central aisle are each 72 feet (22 m) high. Behind
four more pylons lies the sanctuary area. Another
series of pylons and courtyards joins on from the
south. In one courtyard 751 stone statues and stelae
and 17,000 bronze figurines were found buried.

The other main buildings at Karnak include
temples to the Theban god Montu and the creator
god Ptah. Separate temples were built for Mut, the
consort of Amon, and for Khons, their son. The
temple of Mut once held more than 700 granite
statues of the fierce lioness goddess Mut-Sekhmet.
These statues, carved under Amenhotep III, were
thought to protect Egypt from invasions and plagues.
A wonderful statue of a queen of Amenhotep III has
recently been found in this temple.

▲ An avenue of sphinxes
linked Karnak to a canal. Each
statue shows Amon as a ram-
headed lion with a king
between his front paws.

▼ The massive columns of the Great Hypostyle Hall at Karnak
temple. The hall dates to the 13th century B.C.E. Most of the
columns were toppled by earthquakes and had to be re-
erected in the 19th century C.E.

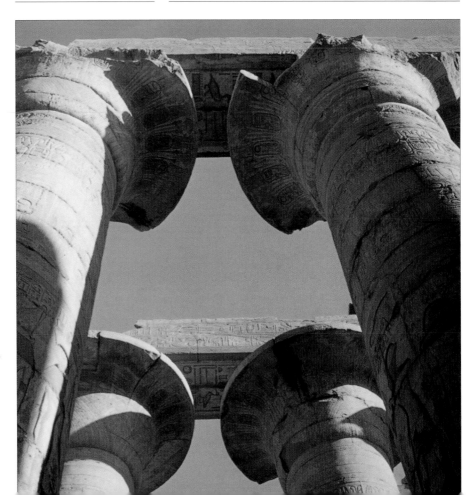

Thebes • West Bank Sites

Temples and tombs of the city of the dead

AFTER KING MENTUHOTEP REUNITED EGYPT in 2040 B.C.E., he built himself a tomb and temple on the west bank at Deir el-Bahri. Nearly 600 years later Queen Hatshepsut built her beautiful temple against the dramatic cliffs of Deir el-Bahri. Thutmose III also built here, but his temple has been badly damaged by repeated rock falls.

Later kings built monuments closer to the edge of the floodplain. Two huge statues known as the Colossi of Memnon mark the mortuary temple of Amonhotep III. The temple of Ramesses II is called the Ramesseum. In 1165 B.C.E. necropolis workmen demonstrated outside this temple in a dispute over wages. This is the earliest known strike.

A whole town grew up around the great temple of Ramesses III at Medinet Habu, the best-preserved mortuary temple of Thebes. The king was nearly the victim of a murder plot while staying in a palace next to the temple. Because of its strong fortifications, Medinet Habu became a refuge in chaotic times.

▶ Two men pick grapes in a vine arbor—one of the many vivid scenes from daily life painted on the walls of 18th-Dynasty Theban tombs. The men would then crush the grapes by treading on them in a vat and use the liquid to make wine.

▶ The Colossi of Memnon are statues of Amonhotep III. They are nearly 60 ft (18 m) high. After the northern statue was damaged in an earthquake in 27 B.C.E., it made a strange sound at dawn. This "singing" stopped when the statue was repaired in the third century C.E.

▶ Funeral scenes are also common in Theban tombs. Here a mummy fitted with a mask is carried by four men. A fifth man burns incense in an arm-shaped holder.

Tombs in the city of the dead

All kinds of people were buried in tombs in the Theban necropolis. One 11th-Dynasty tomb held the bodies of 60 soldiers killed in battle. New Kingdom craftsmen often took time off from royal projects to decorate their own tombs. Whereas the paintings and reliefs in the royal tombs usually depicted traditional rituals, the art in the private tombs often represented everyday life.

The so-called Tombs of the Nobles are those of high officials. Many contain wonderful paintings or reliefs. Some of these tombs are unfinished because their owners suddenly fell from royal favor.

Members of the royal family were buried in the Valley of the Queens. The finest tomb there belongs to Queen Nefertari. Its paintings were badly damaged by rock salt but have been restored to their full beauty.

The royal mummies

In the Valley of the Kings 63 tombs have been found. In most, rock-cut passages and stairways lead past one or more halls to the burial chamber. The walls are decorated with religious scenes. The most elaborate tombs are those of Seti I and Ramesses VI.

Each king was buried with a fortune in funerary goods. By the end of the New Kingdom most of the tombs in the valley had been robbed. Under the 21st Dynasty many of the royal mummies were moved to a secret hiding place, where they lay undiscovered until 1881. The great New Kingdom rulers now rest in the Egyptian Museum in Cairo.

▶ A painted relief in the tomb of Horemheb in the Valley of the Kings. This tomb was designed to foil thieves. The first room was made to look like a dead-end by concealing the door to the next room behind a solid-looking decorated wall. In the second room the stairway to the burial chamber was hidden under the floor. In spite of these tricks, the tomb was soon robbed of its treasure.

The Treasures of Tutankhamon

THE MOST FAMOUS TOMB IN THE VALLEY of the Kings is that of Tutankhamon. Little is known about this short-lived ruler. He was probably the son of Akhenaten by a lesser wife called Kiya. As a boy his name was Tutankhaten. The throne passed to Tutankhaten around 1333 B.C.E., when he was about seven years old. The boy king was married to one of the six daughters of Akhenaten and his chief wife Nefertiti.

After a few years at el-Amarna, the court returned to Thebes and Memphis. Akhenaten's new capital and religion were both abandoned. Amon became the chief god of Egypt again and the king changed his name from Tutankhaten to Tutankhamon. Only 10 years after he came to the throne Tutankhamon died. The cause of death is uncertain, but it may have been a head injury.

A hasty burial

Because of the king's early death, his tomb in the Valley of the Kings was not ready to be occupied. A small tomb that had probably been cut for the vizier Aya was hastily decorated in preparation for a royal burial. A huge quantity of precious objects was crammed into its four rooms.

Shortly after the burial two attempts were made to rob the tomb. The fingerprints of one of the thieves are still visible inside an ointment jar. Necropolis guards discovered the crimes before much was taken, however. The tomb was quickly tidied up and then resealed. Its entrance was probably soon hidden by landslips. Rubble from building work on the nearby tomb of Ramesses VI buried the entrance still deeper.

The discovery of the tomb

In 1917 an English Egyptologist named Howard Carter began excavating in the Valley of the Kings. No unrobbed royal burial had ever been found in the valley, but Tutankhamon's tomb was still unlocated. With financial support from his patron, Lord Carnarvon, Carter spent six digging seasons searching for the tomb. He almost gave up but in November 1922 he found a rock-cut step. A stairway leading down to a sealed entrance was quickly uncovered. Lord Carnarvon hurried out to Egypt for the opening of the tomb. The doorway had the unbroken seals of ancient necropolis guards.

The four chambers were revealed, each filled with various treasures buried with the young king to provide for his needs in the afterlife. The first chamber to be examined was an anteroom crowded

◀ This photograph, taken shortly after the opening of Tutankhamon's tomb, reveals part of the antechamber. It shows how the treasures were piled together to fit into a small space. A new tomb containing seven coffins has recently been found close to the tomb of Tutankhamon.

▶ A tender scene adorning part of the golden throne of Tutankhamon. The young king is shown in a relaxed pose. Queen Ankhesenamon, his wife, rubs scented oil into his jeweled collar. The throne is made from gold-plated wood decorated with silver and gold leaf, semiprecious stones, and glass.

▼ The funeral procession of Tutankhamon. The royal coffins, weighing more than 2,900 lb (1,315 kg), lie on a frame inside a bark (boat) shrine. The shrine, mounted on a sled, is dragged along by courtiers and a team of oxen. The courtiers wear white headbands, a sign of mourning. Next comes an alabaster shrine shouldered by priests. This holds the four canopic jars containing the liver, lungs, stomach, and intestines of the king.

with marvelous objects. There were statues and chariots and animal-shaped beds. The furniture included thrones, stools, chests, and painted boxes. Among the smaller items found were alabaster vases, golden jewelry, gloves, sandals, riding crops, bronze trumpets, and ostrich-feather fans.

The golden treasures

Two life-size statues guarded the main burial chamber. The burial chamber itself was filled by four gilded shrines. Inside the innermost shrine was the red sandstone sarcophagus of Tutankhamon. The mummy was protected by a set of three coffins. Between the coffins were the dried remains of garlands of olive and willow leaves and lotus flowers. Carter was amazed to find that the third coffin was made from 296 troy pounds (110 kg) of gold. Inside this coffin was the mummy itself, its head covered in a beautiful golden portrait mask.

The body of Tutankhamon was in bad condition because too many ointments had been used on it. The king's vital organs were stored in an alabaster chest in another room. It took about 10 years of careful work to clear the tomb of all its treasures. Most of the objects are on display in the Egyptian Museum in Cairo.

Northern Upper Egypt

NORTHERN UPPER EGYPT WAS THE heartland of ancient Egypt. The Badarian/Tasian and Naqada cultures, from which Egyptian civilization developed, are named after sites in this area. The presence of gold in the Eastern Desert was a vital factor in the rise of an early kingdom centered on Northern Upper Egypt. Just as important as gold were trade routes from this area to the Red Sea, particularly the Wadi Hammamat.

Gold mines and stone quarries lay along this wadi, and dismantled ships were carried through it on the 100-mile (160-km) journey to the Red Sea coast. Ship parts and cargo boxes dating back 4,000 years have recently been found in caves on this coast. When the ships were put together again they sailed north to carry turquoise miners to Sinai or south to Yemen or Punt (possibly modern-day Eritrea) to fetch spices and incense.

A holy place

Another site that began to be important in early times was Abydos. Some Predynastic kings and most First- and Second-Dynasty rulers had tombs close to Abydos at Umm el-Qaab. Abydos was a religious rather than a political center. Its main god was Khentamentiu (Chief of the Westerners). The Westerners were the spirits of the dead who had reached the Egyptian paradise—"The Beautiful West." From the late Old Kingdom, Khentamentiu was identified with the god Osiris.

In the Middle and New Kingdoms Abydos was the most important of the places that claimed to be the burial place of Osiris. Every year the story of how Osiris was murdered and brought back to life was acted out. This festival attracted pilgrims from all over the country. Every Egyptian hoped to visit Abydos at least once in a lifetime. It was common to depict the journey in tomb decoration, so that a person could make the journey after death if it had not been possible during life.

It was also thought that anyone who had built a tomb or a monument at Abydos would share in the resurrection of Osiris. Some kings built mortuary temples in which offerings were made to their spirits. Even ordinary people put up stelae or cenotaphs so that their spirits could join with Osiris in his triumph over death.

The shadow of Thebes

From the Middle Kingdom onwards the growth of Thebes overshadowed all the other towns in Northern Upper Egypt. New Kingdom rulers did build temples at Abydos, Koptos, and Dendara, but the temples of Thebes were larger and richer. Thebes remained the most important political and religious center in the area until the end of the Late Period.

Under Greek and Roman rule other towns flourished. There are fine temples dating to the Greco-Roman Period at sites such as Dendara, Nag el-Madamud, Akhmim, and Hiw. These temples usually replaced earlier, simpler buildings. The god Min was worshiped at Koptos for 3,500 years and his temple was rebuilt many times during that period. Among the objects found in this temple were three figures of Min which are the oldest colossal stone statues in the world.

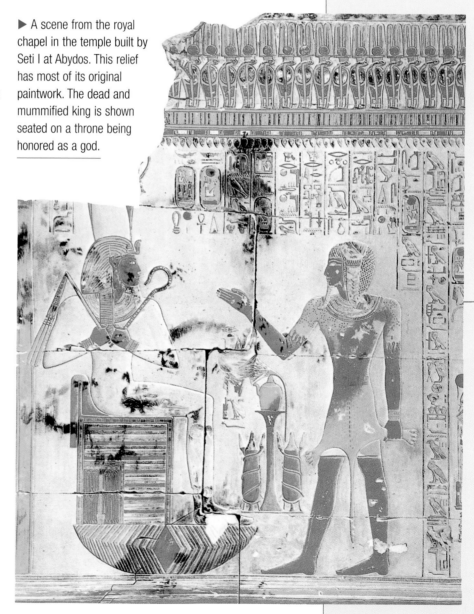

▶ A scene from the royal chapel in the temple built by Seti I at Abydos. This relief has most of its original paintwork. The dead and mummified king is shown seated on a throne being honored as a god.

Amarna

B

C

MIDDLE EGYPT
SEE PAGE 75

Manfalut

Asyut
(Lykopolis)

NORTHERN

el-Badari

Tima

Qaw el-Kebir (Antaeopolis)

UPPER

Sohagiya Canal

Tahta

Nile

el-Maragha

EGYPT

Akhmim (Panopolis)

Sohag

Wannina (Athribis)

Girga (Thinis)

(Abydos)

Umm el-Qaab

3

2

▲ The ruins of the Greco-Roman temple of Montu at Nag el-Madamud. There was a temple on this site from the early Middle Kingdom. Montu was a hawk-headed god, but his sacred animal was a bull. These bulls were kept in a separate temple.

Eastern Desert

Qena (Kaine)

Dendara
(Iunet)

Nag Hammadi Barrage

el-Qasr wa'l - Saiyad
(Khenoboskion)

Hiw (Diospolis Parva)

Qift (Koptos)

Naqada
(Ombos/Nubt)

Qus (Apollinopolis Parva)

Western Desert

Types of ancient site

Symbol	Description
▲	Major town
●	Other modern town
•	Location of ancient site
– – –	Regional boundary
	Road
▮	Fertile land

Types of ancient site
▲ Pyramid
◯ Settlement
▼ Temple
◼ Tomb
◆ Other

Qus   Modern name
(Iunet) Ancient name

Scale 1 : 1 000 000

0   30 km
0   20 miles

Valley of the Kings

Nag el-Madamud

Luxor
(Thebes)

Tod

SOUTHERN
UPPER
EGYPT
SEE PAGE 59

Gebelein (Per-Hathor)

Esna (Latopolis)

Nile

1

Northern Upper Egypt • Sites

Dendara temples

DENDARA WAS AN IMPORTANT TOWN IN the Old Kingdom and the First Intermediate Period. It was the main cult center of Hathor, who was a goddess of birth and death. She was also linked with love, music, foreign lands, and precious minerals.

Every year the cult statue of Hathor made the journey from Dendara to Edfu for the festival of her "marriage" to Horus. Hathor, Horus, and their son Ihy each had their own temple at Dendara. Only the temple complex of Hathor still stands.

The sacred area

Inside the enclosure wall of the Hathor temple is a sacred lake. Priests washed in such lakes in order to make themselves pure before entering a sanctuary. Among the buildings surrounding the Hathor temple are a sanatorium and two "birth houses." Sick people slept in the sanatorium. They hoped that Hathor would tell them in a dream how they could be cured. Patients also drank or bathed in sacred water.

A birth house is a shrine celebrating the birth of a deity. At Dendara reliefs in the two birth houses show Hathor giving birth to her son. Women prayed to Hathor, Lady of Dendara, to bring them safely through the ordeal of childbirth.

The temple of Hathor

The temple of Hathor was built and decorated between the second century B.C.E. and the first century C.E. It has two splendid columned halls. Several shrines were also built on top of the flat roof. The roof is one of very few remaining ceiling structures in ancient Egyptian temples.

Sacred treasures were once hidden in small underground rooms near the sanctuary. On the rear wall of the temple Cleopatra VII appears with her son by Julius Caesar (see page 46). In the middle of this wall is a huge symbol of Hathor. Most visitors prayed to the goddess at this spot.

▶ The outer columned hall at Dendara. Four faces of the goddess Hathor form the capital to each of the columns. The artists used wooden scaffolding and worked from the top downward.

Temples and tombs at Abydos

A MIDDLE KINGDOM AND SECOND Intermediate Period town has been excavated in the southern part of Abydos. Little of the main temple of Osiris, which was in central Abydos, survives. The necropolis of Abydos spreads for about 1 mile (1.6 km) along the desert edge. The first burials were made there in the fourth millennium B.C.E.

The Mother of Pots

The earliest royal tombs at Abydos resemble underground palaces with brick-lined rooms. They are near the area known as Umm el-Qaab and date to the little-known Dynasty O. Some First-Dynasty kings built tombs at Umm el-Qaab and huge brick enclosures nearer to the town. The tomb of King Djer was later thought to be the burial place of Osiris.

Umm el-Qaab means "Mother of Pots." It gets its name from the thousands of pottery fragments left by pilgrims to what was then believed to be the tomb of Osiris. Stone slabs (stelae) and cenotaphs (empty tombs) were set up along the route from this holy place to the main temple of Osiris.

The temple of Seti I

Several kings built mortuary temples in the southern part of Abydos. By far the best preserved of these is the temple of King Seti I, known as the Memnonium. It is built in fine white limestone. Originally there were two pylons, two courtyards, and two columned halls. The plan of the inner area is unique. It has seven sanctuaries side by side.

One sanctuary was for the cult of Seti himself. Another is dedicated to Osiris. Its walls are decorated with scenes from the myth of Osiris. A group of rooms for the worship of Osiris, Isis, and Horus opens off this sanctuary. The reliefs here are among the most delicate and beautiful in all Egyptian art. They depict ceremonies associated with the gods. In another part of the temple, Seti is shown with his heir Ramesses II making offerings to a list of royal ancestors. Ramesses completed his father's temple and built his own nearby.

Behind the temple of Seti I is a mysterious building known as the Osireion. It was probably begun under Seti I and finished by his grandson Merneptah. The main feature was an underground hall built in red granite. An artificial island was constructed in the middle of the hall and a canal dug to surround the island with water. A sarcophagus was placed on the island. This building could be a dummy royal tomb, a model of the tomb of Osiris, or a re-creation of the first mound of land rising above the waters of chaos.

▼ A painted relief from the temple of Ramesses II at Abydos. Animals such as fattened oxen are led in to be sacrificed to the gods. Major temples had their own slaughterhouses. After the joints of meat had been offered to the gods, they were shared out among the priests as part of their wages. At a festival, more than 100 animals might be killed in a day to feed the visiting crowds.

▲ Ivory comb from the tomb of King Wadj/Djet at Abydos, dating back to the Early Dynastic Period. Hieroglyphic inscriptions on recent finds from royal tombs at Abydos have pushed back the date for the invention of writing to around 3200 B.C.E.

Middle Egypt

THE TERM MIDDLE EGYPT DESCRIBES SOME 180 miles (290 km) of the Nile valley from Asyut to Memphis. It also includes the Faiyum, a large area of fertile land jutting out into the Western Desert. A branch of the Nile River flowed through the Faiyum into Lake Moeris. This lake was much bigger in ancient times than it is today.

Royal tombs and cities

Middle Egypt has few large temples, but it does have many interesting tombs. Some kings were buried in this area. There is a Third/Fourth Dynasty royal pyramid at Maidum, and Middle Kingdom rulers built pyramids at el-Lisht, el-Lahun, and Hawara.

These 12th-Dynasty pyramids were poorly constructed and are now in ruins. The vast mortuary temple of Amenemhet III at Hawara was famous in the ancient world as "The Labyrinth." Almost nothing of it survives. Nor has any trace been found of the 12th-Dynasty capital Itjtawy, which lay somewhere near el-Lisht. In the 18th Dynasty another capital city and royal necropolis was built in Middle Egypt at el-Amarna.

The nomarchs of Middle Egypt

From the Sixth Dynasty to the late 12th Dynasty the nomarchs of Middle Egypt enjoyed much power and independence. They built splendid rock-cut tombs and were buried in coffins painted with maps of the underworld. The nomarchs of Herakleopolis called themselves kings in the First Intermediate Period.

Both Herakleopolis and Hermopolis were the capital towns of some minor kings during the Third Intermediate Period.

Known to the Egyptians as The City of the Eight (meaning eight gods), Hermopolis was located on the west bank of the Nile River between Thebes and Memphis. It was the main cult center of the god Thoth, the god of the moon, wisdom, and writing. A huge temple complex once stood here. Among the surviving monuments are two colossal statues of Thoth as a baboon. Sacred baboons and ibises, the bird of Thoth, were buried in underground galleries in the necropolis at Tuna el-Gebel. This necropolis has painted tombs of the Greco-Roman Period.

▲ A blue faience hippopotamus from a tomb at Meir. The body is decorated with marsh plants. This charming figurine dates to the late 20th century B.C.E. Model animals have been found in many Middle Kingdom tombs.

◄ A Middle Kingdom temple at Qasr el-Sagha in the desert north of the Faiyum. In ancient times part of Lake Moeris reached almost to this site. Most of the monuments in the Faiyum area date to the Middle Kingdom or the Greco-Roman Period. Crocodiles were once common in Lake Moeris. When Egyptians had to cross water they chanted spells against being snatched by a crocodile.

SEE ALSO
PAGES 88–89

• Qasr el-Sagha

▼

el-Lisht (Itjtawy) •
▲ ■

Birket Qarun
(Lake Moeris)

Maidum •
▲ ■

Atfih •
(Aphroditopolis)

Seila •
◆

Medinet el-Faiyum (Krokodilopolis) •

el-Wasta •

FAIYUM

Hawara •
▲ ■

el-Lahun •
▲

Kom Medinet Ghurab •
■

Sidmant el-Gebel •
■

Ihnasya el-Medina (Herakleopolis) •
■

Beni Suef ●

Western Desert

el-Fashn •

el-Hiba (Ankyronon Polis) •
▼

MIDDLE **EGYPT**

el-Bahnasa (Oxyrhynchus) •
● ■

Beni Mazar •

Samalut •

Tihna (Akoris) •
● ▼

el-Minya (Menat-Khufu) •
◆

Zawyet el-Amwat •
▲

Beni Hasan •

(Speos Artemidos) •
▼

el-Ashmunein (Hermopolis) •

Tuna el-Gebel (Hermopolis) •
■

Deir el-Bersha •
■

Mallawi •

el-Sheikh Said •
■

el-Amarna (Akhetaten) •
▼

SEE PAGE 78
FOR MORE DETAIL

Dairut •

Meir (Cusae) •

el-Qusiya (Cusae) •

Deir el-Gabrawi •
■

Manfalut •

Abnub •

Sohagiya Canal

Nile

Asyut ●

Asyut •
(Lykopolis)

**NORTHERN
UPPER EGYPT**
SEE PAGES 70–71

Legend

◆ Major town
● Other modern town
• Location of ancient site
– – – Regional boundary
═══ Road
▨ Fertile land

Types of ancient site
▲ Pyramid
● Settlement
▼ Temple
■ Tomb
◆ Other

Meir Modern name
(Cusae) Ancient name

Scale 1 : 1 000 000

0 ———— 30 km
0 ———— 20 miles

3

2

1

A

B

75

Meir

MEIR IS THE SITE OF THE NECROPOLIS for the ancient town of Cusae, of which nothing survives. The town, about 30 miles (50 km) northwest of Asyut, was the administrative center of a nome. The rock-cut tombs at Meir belong to nomarchs of the Sixth and 12th Dynasties.

Each tomb consists of a large room cut inside the cliff face. There are niches for statues and offerings and deep shafts for the coffins. The walls are decorated with painted reliefs. Hunting in the desert and fishing in the marshes are common scenes. Other themes include vase-making and harvesting.

A festival associated with Hathor is illustrated in several of the tombs. The late 12th-Dynasty tomb of Wekh-hotep has some of the most delicate paintings to survive from the Middle Kingdom. They show the nomarch spearing fish and throwing a boomerang at marsh birds.

▼ A family group from a late 12th-Dynasty tomb at Meir. The nomarch (local ruler) Wekh-hotep is shown with his two wives and a small daughter.

Maidum

MAIDUM IS THE SITE OF A MYSTERIOUS building disaster. A curious tower rising from a mound of rubble is all that remains of an early attempt to build a true pyramid. The original size of the pyramid was 472 feet (144 m) square and 138 feet (42 m) high. It was probably begun for Huni, the last king of the Third Dynasty, and completed by his successor Snofru.

The Maidum pyramid started as a seven-stepped structure. Then an eighth step was built. The steps were filled in and a limestone casing was added to create a smooth-sided pyramid. This outer casing was not well laid and it had no proper foundations. As a result, the pyramid collapsed. It is not clear, however, whether this happened just after the pyramid was finished or hundreds of years later. Close to the pyramid are some early Fourth-Dynasty *mastaba* (flat-roofed) tombs.

▼ A view of the tower-shaped core of the collapsed pyramid at Maidum. It stands on a "hill" formed by stone debris. A causeway runs up to a small temple on the east side of the pyramid. This was where offerings were made to the dead king.

Beni Hasan

▲ The rubble core of the Maidum pyramid is now visible in places. When the foundations collapsed, the outer walls slid down to form a tower shape.

▼ A section showing the three stages of the Maidum pyramid:
1 Seven-stepped pyramid.
2 Eight-stepped pyramid.
3 True geometric pyramid.

DECORATED ROCK-CUT TOMBS BELONGING to Middle Egyptian nomarchs survive at sites at Asyut, Deir el-Gabrawi, Meir, el-Sheikh Said, Deir el-Bersha, and Beni Hasan. The most interesting are the group at Beni Hasan. There are 39 tombs here, dating from the 11th to the late 12th Dynasties. Wooden coffins, statuettes, and models have been found in them. The more elaborate tombs have an outer court and portico and a rock-cut main room with elegant pillars. The decoration on the walls is painted rather than carved.

The ceilings, too, are painted with geometric patterns to imitate matting or textiles. Scenes from daily life cover most of the wall space. Unusual paintings of battles and sieges illustrate wars between nomes. Gentler scenes include girls playing ball, men and baboons harvesting figs, and the arrival of a group of traders from Palestine. The paintings have recently been restored.

In a nearby valley, about 0.9 miles (1.5 km) to the south of Beni Hasan, Queen Hatshepsut built a small temple. This unfinished rock-cut temple is known as Speos Artemidos. It was dedicated to a lioness goddess called Pakhet. Her name means "she who scratches."

▼ A model boat made from wood and linen. It comes from a 12th-Dynasty tomb at Benl Hasan. A mummy is shown on deck on a bier (a funerary bed) under a canopy. The dead person is being taken to Abydos to share in the death and rebirth of Osiris. The model boat was thought to make this journey by magic. There was then no need for the real mummy to be taken to Abydos. Model boats have been found in many rock-cut tombs in Middle Egypt.

Middle Egypt 2

City of el-Amarna

O NE OF ANCIENT EGYPT'S GREAT CITIES
was el-Amarna in Middle Egypt, but only for
15 years. Its Egyptian name was Akhetaten
(The Horizon of the Sun Disk). When the pharaoh
Akhenaten decided to build a new capital he chose
a site that had never been inhabited before on a flat
stretch of land beside the Nile valley. Work began in
haste in about 1349 B.C.E. and the city spread rapidly
to cover an area of about 2 square miles (5 sq. km).
The city's population is estimated to have been
about 30,000 or more.

Palaces, temples, and tombs

The city of el-Amarna became the chief royal
residence and the center of government. There were
at least five palaces, many official buildings, several

▲ Plan of the areas of
el-Amarna excavated so
far. The temples and altars
marked were all dedicated
to the Sun Disk (Aten). The
purpose of some buildings,
such as the Maru Aten, is
uncertain. The workmen's
village continued to be lived
in for some time after the
main city was abandoned.

◀ This picture shows what
part of the central city would
have looked like c.1340 B.C.E.
The King's Way was 130 ft
(40 m) wide. It passed under
the King's Bridge, linking the
Great Palace to Akhenaten's
private apartments (the King's
House). The Great Palace had
a series of stone courts and
halls. The Royal Temple, built
for the Aten, was the second
largest in the city.

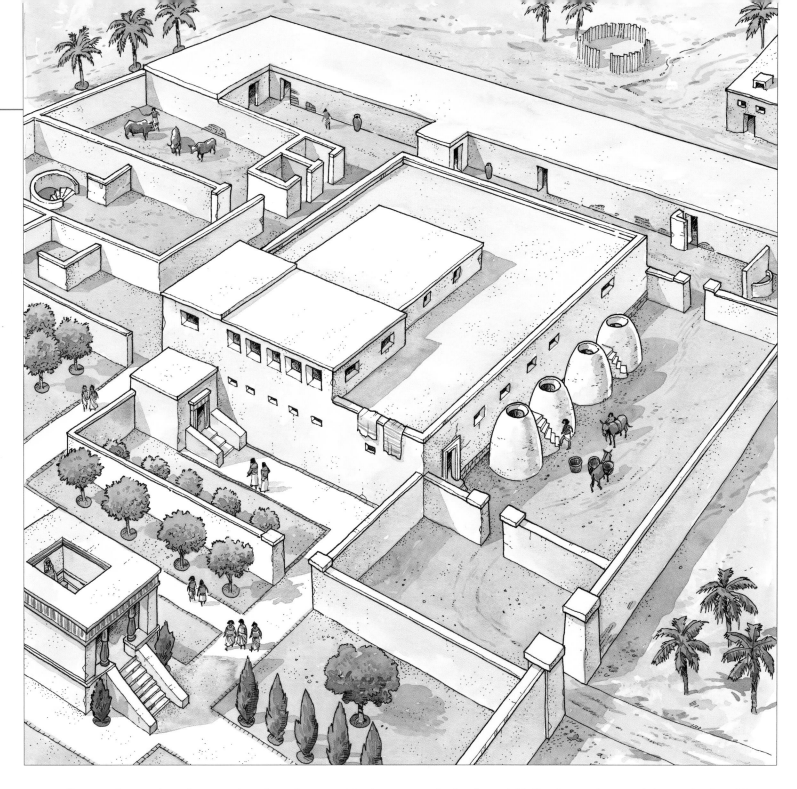

necropolises, and a number of zoos and gardens. In the mud-brick palaces walls, floors, and ceilings were painted or tiled in brilliant colors. One room in the North Palace had a marvelous painting of birds in a papyrus thicket covering three walls. Akhenaten's private apartments were decorated with charming pictures of Queen Nefertiti and the little princesses. Great officials such as the vizier also had finely decorated homes at el-Amarna.

The only deities worshiped at el-Amarna were the Aten (the Sun Disk) and Akhenaten himself. A new type of temple was built for the Aten. Unlike temples to other Egyptian gods, these temples had huge courtyards with hundreds of altars open to the sun.

Tombs were cut in the desert hills for the royal family and favored courtiers. Most were never used. Their reliefs represented the official view of life in el-Amarna. In many scenes the rays of the Sun Disk end in hands holding out the symbol of life to Akhenaten.

The deserted city
Akhenaten's new ideas were not popular. After his death people called him "The Great Criminal." During Tutankhamon's reign the city was deserted and never lived in again. Everything of value was taken away. Portraits of the disgraced royal family, including the famous head of Nefertiti (see page 18), were left behind in a sculptor's workshop.

▲ A reconstruction of the villa of a high official at el-Amarna. Such villas were like miniature farms. Fruit and vegetables were grown in the gardens. There were beehive-shaped grain bins (center right), a cattle yard, and stalls and stables for chariot horses. Each villa had a shrine for worship of the Aten and the royal family (bottom left).

Memphis

MEMPHIS WAS THE FIRST CAPITAL OF ALL Egypt. For 3,000 years it was one of the country's greatest cities, but little of that greatness survives. Most of Memphis is now buried deep under Nile silt or modern settlements. Remains of a few of the major buildings of Memphis can be seen in the palm groves around the village of Mit Rahina. A huge statue of Ramesses II still lies where it was found. A museum has been built around it.

The chief deity of Memphis was the creator god Ptah. Only a small part of the temple complex of Ptah has been excavated. It was one of the largest temples in Egypt. Many kings were crowned there, including Alexander the Great. Palaces belonging to 19th- and 26th-Dynasty kings have been found at Mit Rahina.

A sacred bull

The god Ptah was represented by a sacred bull known as the Apis Bull. An Apis Bull had to have a white triangle on a black forehead, a scarab shape under its tongue, and 27 other special marks on its body. The bull was kept in great luxury and led in procession once a year at the festival of "The Running of the Apis Bull." When the bull died, it was mummified and placed in a huge stone sarcophagus.

From the time of Ramesses II the bulls were buried in underground galleries at Saqqara, part of the necropolis for Memphis. Above the galleries developed a temple known as the Serapeum. From the third century B.C.E. the chief god of this temple was Serapis, who was created from Greek and Egyptian deities.

Cows who had given birth to Apis Bulls, as well as sacred dogs, cats, and ibises were also buried at Saqqara. Paying for the mummification and burial of a temple animal was thought to please the gods. Archaeologists exploring one set of galleries found the mummified bodies of more than 2 million sacred ibises. In ancient Egypt the ibis was seen as an incarnation of the god Thoth.

The great necropolis

The necropolis for Memphis stretches for 18 miles (30 km) along the edge of the Western Desert from Dahshur to Abu Rawash. It is probably the largest cemetery in the world, reflecting the importance of the city itself. Besides the pyramids at Giza, there are about 50 smaller tombs. Among the royal tombs are step pyramids and true pyramids. From the Fourth Dynasty each pyramid had two attached temples.

The valley temple was built on the edge of the floodplain so that it could be reached by boat. From the valley temple the royal coffin was taken up an enclosed causeway to the mortuary temple. This was usually on the east side of the pyramid because the king hoped that he would be reborn, like the sun rising in the east. Priests made offerings to the king's spirit in the mortuary temple. Sometimes this cult would continue for hundreds of years after a king had died. Towns were built to house the priests who served the dead kings.

Small subsidiary pyramids were also part of a pyramid complex. By the Middle Kingdom they were used for the burial of royal ladies. In the Old Kingdom some may have been for the king's vital organs. The *mastaba* tombs of high officials and members of the royal family are grouped around the Old Kingdom pyramids.

◄ A bronze statuette of an Apis Bull. Many bronze figures of deities were presented to temples by pious Egyptians during the Late and Greco-Roman Periods.

▼ Tomb types in the Memphis necropolis:
1 *Mastaba* tomb, First–Sixth Dynasties.
2 Step pyramid, Third Dynasty.
3 Bent pyramid, Fourth Dynasty.
4 True pyramid, Old and Middle Kingdoms.

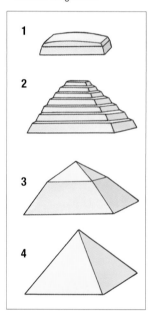

◄ One of the underground galleries of the Serapeum at Saqqara. The niches in the walls once held stelae left by pilgrims. About 1,200 of these stelae survive. The pilgrims came to take part in the burial rites of the Apis Bull and other sacred animals. Pilgrims who paid for the burial of a temple animal were often cheated by the embalmers, who bandaged up a few stray bones instead of a whole corpse.

Nile

Tell Hisn
(Heliopolis)

Ard el-Naam

Ausim
(Letopolis)

el-Matariya

el-Zeitan

Heliopolis

Warraq el-Hadf

el-Sharabiya

Warraq el-Arab

Shubra

Medinet Nasr

el-Muhit Idku el-Gharbi

el-Mohandissin

CAIRO

Gebel Ahmar

Nahya

Wadi Qaren

Abu Rawash

el-Doqqi

▲ Radjedef

Kirdasa

Saft el-Laban

Gebel Muqattam

Old Cairo
(Babylon)

Medinet
el-Muqattam

el-Giza

Eastern Desert

el-Tabliya

Nazlet el-Samman

Khufu (Great Pyramid)

West Field ▲ ■ East Field
Khephren ▲
Menkaura ▲ ▲ Great Sphinx

el-Basalin

**GIZA
PYRAMIDS**

el-Harraniya

Abu el-Numrus

Maadi

Wadi Digla

**ZAWYET EL-ARYAN
PYRAMIDS**

? (Unfinished Pyramid) ▲

Zawyet
el-Aryan

Shabramant

Tura ◆

Gebel Tura

Khaba? (Layer Pyramid) ▲

Western Desert

Mit Qadus

Gebel Hof

Bahr el-Libeini

Umm Khunan

el-Masara

ABU GHURAB TEMPLES

Sun Temple of Neuserra ▽

Abu Ghurab

Sun Temple of Userkaf ▽ ▲ Sahura
▲ Neuserra

el-Omari

Raneferef? ▲
Neferirkara ▲

ABUSIR PYRAMIDS

Abusir

(Serapeum) ▲ Teti ▲ Merykara?

MEMPHIS
(Mennufer)

Djoser (Step Pyramid) ▲
Great Enclosure ◆ ▲ Userkaf

Palace of Apries

Wenis ▲
Sekhemkhet ▲ ■ Horemheb

Northern Enclosure

Great Temple of Ptah Enclosure

Helwan ■

**SAQQARA
PYRAMIDS**

Pepy I ▲
Merenra ▲ ▲ Izezi

Mit Rahina

Saqqara

Palace of Merneptah

Helwan

Pepy II ▲ ▲ Ibi

Khendjer ▲

Senwosret III ▲

el-Tabbin

Snofru
(Red Pyramid) ▲

Amenemhet II
(White Pyramid) ▲

DAHSHUR PYRAMIDS

Minshat Dahshur

Snofru
(Bent Pyramid) ▲

Amenemhet III
(Black Pyramid) ▲

Wadi el-Garawi

**MAZGHUNA
PYRAMIDS**

▲ ?
▲ ?

Zawyet
Dahshur

Nile

Types of ancient site

▲ Pyramid (with related
temples and tombs)

○ Settlement

▽ Temple

■ Tomb

◆ Other

Built up area

● Other modern town

Road

Fertile land

Tura Modern name
(Babylon) Ancient name

Scale 1:150 000

0 ———————— 4 km

0 ———————— 3 miles

Dahshur

DAHSHUR IS THE SOUTHERNMOST PART OF the necropolis of Memphis. Snofru, the first king of the Fourth Dynasty, built two stone pyramids here. They are known as the Bent Pyramid and the Red Pyramid.

The Bent Pyramid

The Bent Pyramid was probably the first royal tomb that was designed as a true pyramid. When it was half built, the angle of the outer faces was suddenly reduced to give a gentler slope. At the same time, a new method of laying the casing stones was introduced. These changes may have been made in order to prevent this pyramid collapsing like the one at Maidum (see page 76). The Red Pyramid (named for the red limestone used in its construction) is a huge true pyramid built at the same angle as the upper part of the Bent Pyramid.

Royal treasures

Three 12th-Dynasty rulers—Amenemhet II, Senwosret III, and Amenemhet III—built stone-faced, mud-brick pyramids at Dahshur. Two minor 13th-Dynasty kings were buried nearby. Six wooden boats were found in a pit near the pyramid of Senwosret III.

The tombs of queens and princesses are grouped around the 12th-Dynasty pyramids. Wonderful jewelry has been recovered from seven of the burials. The royal ladies had crowns, necklaces, pendants, bracelets, and anklets. They were made in gold, lapis lazuli, turquoise, amethyst, and cornelian. Most of them are now in the Egyptian Museum at Cairo.

▲ Wooden statue of a king's *ka* (spirit) from a 13th-Dynasty tomb at Dahshur. The pair of arms on the head is the *ka* sign.

▼ The Bent Pyramid (left) and the Red Pyramid (far right) at Dahshur. In the foreground are two Old Kingdom royal tombs at Saqqara—showing how close together the two royal cemeteries are.

Saqqara

SAQQARA WAS AN IMPORTANT CEMETERY for more than 3,000 years. Kings were buried here at least as early as the Second Dynasty. The most famous monument is the Step Pyramid (see page 31), but there are 13 other pyramids at Saqqara. They range in date from the Third to the 13th Dynasties.

The writing on the walls

The pyramid of Wenis, the last king of the Fifth Dynasty, is the earliest to be inscribed with the magic spells known as the Pyramid Texts, written on the limestone walls in vertical columns in hieroglyphic script. The spells were probably recited during the funeral. Their purpose was to help the king become a god in the afterlife.

The causeway of this pyramid is decorated with reliefs. There are scenes of boats bringing granite columns from Aswan to Saqqara and workers collecting honey. An inscription records repairs to the pyramid by a son of Ramesses II nearly 1,200 years after it was originally built.

Decorated tombs

From Early Dynastic times high officials were buried in *mastaba* tombs at Saqqara. The finest belong to

◀ This beautifully carved wooden panel from a Saqqara tomb is about 4,600 years old. It shows the "Chief of Dentists and Doctors," called Hezyre.

▶ A tomb statue served as an extra body in case the mummy was destroyed. This statue of a chief priest from Saqqara has inlaid eyes. Plaster and paint would once have covered the wood. Successful men were often shown as middle-aged and fat. Fatness was a symbol of prosperity.

important men of the Fifth and Sixth Dynasties. Their tombs have many small rooms decorated with painted reliefs that show the tomb owner enjoying the good things of life. With 32 rooms, the *mastaba* of the vizier Mereruka is the largest in Saqqara. Scenes in the family tomb show a hippopotamus hunt, girls dancing, children playing leap-frog, and dwarfs walking the household pets. Impressive statues have been found in some of the Old Kingdom tombs.

The next great age of tomb-building at Saqqara was under the late 18th and early 19th Dynasties. High officials of this era had rock-cut tombs or large stone tombs with pillared courts and chapels topped by miniature pyramids. Several New Kingdom tombs with wonderful carved and painted reliefs have been found in the last 20 years.

In the Late Period a new "robber-proof" type of tomb appeared. The coffins were placed at the bottom of large deep shafts, which were then filled with a huge mass of sand.

▲ A Sixth-Dynasty tomb scene shows cattle wading a canal and fish and a hippopotamus below the waterline.

▼ Egyptian guards with an Asiatic prisoner. A scene from the tomb built at Saqqara for Horemheb before he was king.

Buildings at Abusir and Abu Ghurab

THE FOUR FIFTH-DYNASTY PYRAMIDS AT Abusir were not very well constructed. The smooth casing blocks that once hid their rough core masonry have been stripped off to be reused in buildings or made into lime. This has happened to most other Egyptian pyramids.

The pyramid of Sahura

The pyramid complex of King Sahura must have been impressive when it was intact. Most of the reliefs that once decorated its temples have been lost. The few that survive show episodes from royal life. One fragment has the earliest scene of seagoing ships in Egyptian art. Another one shows animals captured during a war with the Libyans. The inscription claims that this booty included as many as 123,440 cattle and 243,688 sheep.

Sahura's successor, Neferirkara, planned a huge pyramid complex at Abusir, but it was never completed. The causeway was taken over by the next king, Neuserra, for his pyramid complex. The fourth Abusir pyramid was built by King Raneferef. The largest of the *mastaba* tombs around these pyramids belonged to the vizier Ptahshepses. Graffiti show that this tomb was a tourist attraction in the New Kingdom. The intact burial of a priest who lived in the Late Period has recently been discovered at Abusir. His mummy was found inside a finely decorated sarcophagus.

Sun temples

Half-way between Abusir and Abu Ghurab, King Userkaf—founder of the Fifth Dynasty—built a great temple to the sun god Ra. This structure has a causeway and a valley temple, making it appear to be a pyramid complex.

At Abu Ghurab a much better-preserved sun temple dates to the reign of Neuserra. Its central feature was an open court with an altar and a giant obelisk built of limestone blocks. The obelisk was a copy of the sacred *benben* stone in the temple of Ra at Heliopolis. This stone was a symbol of the first mound of land and of the rays of the sun. The temple has a huge brick-built model of the boat of the sun god. In the "Room of the Seasons" painted reliefs show giant figures, representing the spirits of inundation, spring, and harvest.

▲ Part of the harvest season relief from the "Room of the Seasons" at Abu Ghurab. In the middle row an oryx is giving birth. At the bottom left are two hunting dogs.

▼ An alabaster (calcite) altar in the open court of the sun temple built by King Neuserra at Abu Ghurab. It is 20 ft (6 m) across. In the distance are three of the Abusir pyramids.

Pyramids at Giza

◀ Part of the valley temple of King Khephren's pyramid complex at Giza. It is built in limestone, alabaster, and polished red granite.

▼ Riders on camels show the massive scale of the Great Pyramid at Giza. A few of the original smooth casing blocks can be seen at the bottom of the pyramid. The Giza pyramids are the only one of the Seven Wonders of the Ancient World that survives.

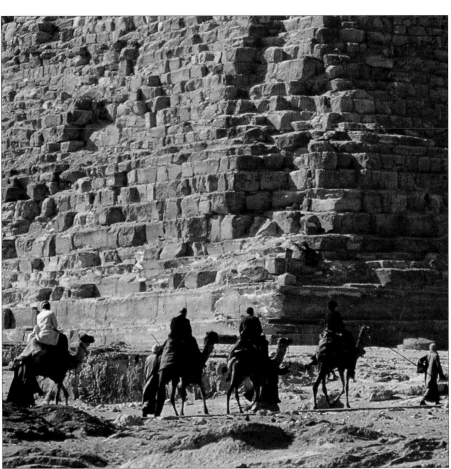

THE PLATEAU OF GIZA LIES ON THE EDGE of modern Cairo. The area was used for burials at least as early as the Second Dynasty. The biggest of all the Egyptian royal tombs were built here during the Fourth Dynasty.

The Great Pyramid

The pyramid of Khufu (Cheops) at Giza is known as the Great Pyramid. Its ancient name was "the Pyramid which is the place of Sunrise and Sunset." The original height was 482 feet (147 m), and it covers an area of 2,800 square yards (2,341 sq. m). Nearly 4,500 years after it was built, it is still one of the world's largest human-made structures. There are five boat pits near this pyramid (see page 52).

Khufu's valley and mortuary temples have not survived. There are three subsidiary pyramids and many stone *mastaba* tombs.

The tomb of Khufu's mother, Queen Hetepheres, lies beside the causeway of the Great Pyramid. The canopic chest holding the queen's vital organs was found in this intact tomb but the sarcophagus was empty. Possibly Hetepheres' original tomb had been robbed and her body destroyed. Among the queen's treasure were 28 silver anklets decorated with butterflies. In the Old Kingdom silver was more valuable than gold.

The second and third pyramids

King Khephren built his pyramid beside that of his father Khufu. His pyramid is only slightly smaller than the Great Pyramid. The third Giza pyramid belongs to King Menkaura. It is much smaller and less impressive than the other two. Beautiful royal statues have been found in the valley temples of Khephren and Menkaura.

Near the valley temple of Khephren an outcrop of limestone was carved into a sphinx 240 feet (73 m) long. The Great Sphinx has the body of a lion and the head of a king—either Khufu or Khephren. In the New Kingdom the Great Sphinx was worshiped as a form of the sun god. Pilgrims left offerings of miniature sphinxes and lions. Close to the Sphinx was a town for the craftsmen who built and decorated the pyramids and their temples. These skilled workers were provided with food, housing, and medical care by the state.

Pyramid Building

BUILDING THE OLD KINGDOM PYRAMIDS was a gigantic task. The Great Pyramid at Giza contains about 7 million tons (6.35 tonnes) of stone. The individual blocks weigh between 2 and 17 tons (1.8–15 tonnes). To complete this pyramid during Khufu's reign, the blocks must have been produced at the rate of one every two minutes each day for 23 years. The stonemasons who quarried, shaped, and smoothed the blocks formed a highly skilled permanent workforce.

Many of the blocks were quarried close to the pyramid site. Granite from Aswan and fine limestone from Tura were brought by barge to the edge of the

▼ Building a pyramid. The central core and the stepped buttress walls can still be seen on this half-finished pyramid. Gangs of men are hauling limestone blocks up the building ramp. Water is poured onto the ropes and sleds to reduce friction (left). To the right, stonemasons check blocks for flatness and two architects are discussing their plan of the pyramid.

desert. The blocks were then lashed on to sleds. They were dragged over wooden rollers, which had to be kept damp to prevent friction. Mud-brick ramps were probably used to get the stones up to where they were needed.

Inside each Old Kingdom pyramid is a series of stepped buttress walls around a central core. Packing blocks were used to fill in the steps. Then the casing stones were added. These were fitted closely to form the smooth outer walls. The casing stones were mainly of pale Tura limestone, so the pyramids

◀ A reconstruction of Sahura's pyramid complex at Abusir. A causeway joins the riverside valley temple to the courtyard of the mortuary temple. There is one subsidiary pyramid.

▼ Sahura's pyramid in a cutaway view. A passage runs from a hidden entrance on the north face to the burial chamber. Some blocks in the roof of this chamber are 36 ft (10 m) long.

would originally have looked white. The capstone at the very top of a pyramid was covered in gold.

Empty burial chambers

The king's burial chamber was usually under the center of the pyramid. In the Great Pyramid the granite burial chamber is reached by a steeply ascending corridor known as the Grand Gallery. After Khufu's funeral, huge granite blocks were slid down to seal off the burial chamber. These precautions failed to stop the tomb robbers. No bodies or treasure have been found in any of the Giza pyramids. New equipment is being used to search the Great Pyramid for hidden chambers.

The Delta

MOST OF THE ANCIENT CITIES OF LOWER Egypt—the Delta—were built on high ground beside branches of the Nile River. The moist climate of the marshy Delta is not good for preserving ancient remains. Unfortunately, many archaeological sites have been lost because the course of river branches and the shape of the coastline have changed over the years.

In more recent times other ancient buildings have been destroyed by people wanting stone for building work or mud-bricks to make into fertilizer. As a result, we know much less about Lower Egypt than we do about Upper Egypt.

Remains of religious sites

The Delta goddess Wadjit was worshiped at Buto for around 3,000 years. The remains of a Predynastic settlement have been found nearly 24 feet (7 m) below the modern surface level at Buto. Changes in the types of pottery and building materials used at this site show that the local culture was gradually overwhelmed by that of Upper Egypt.

Old Kingdom houses and tombs have been found at the important religious sites of Bubastis and Tell el-Ruba (ancient Mendes). Archaeologists working at Mendes have excavated a burned building full of bodies. This may be evidence for a brutal civil war at the end of the Old Kingdom.

Foreign rulers known as the Hyksos seized power in the Delta in the Second Intermediate Period and built the walled city of Avaris (modern Tell el-Daba). The early 18th-Dynasty rulers who defeated the Hyksos put up a new palace at Avaris with wall paintings in Cretan style.

Unrobbed tombs

In the late New Kingdom and for much of the Third Intermediate Period, Egypt was ruled from the Delta. Many kings, princes, and queens were buried inside temple enclosures in Delta cities. Unrobbed royal burials have been found at Tanis and Tell el-Muqdam. Hoards of treasure have also been recovered from the temple area at Bubastis.

The Delta once had temples as impressive as the ones that still stand in southern Egypt. The temple of the goddess Neith at Sais was famous in the ancient world, but little now remains to be seen. Most of the great temple of Ra at Heliopolis is lost beneath the northern suburbs of Cairo. An earthquake seems to have caused the collapse of the unique granite temple of Isis at Behbeit el-Hagar.

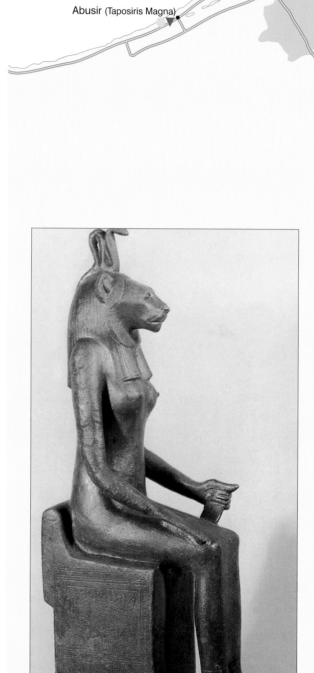

Mediterranean Sea

Rosetta Mouth

Rose

Alexandria (Raqote)

Lake Idku

Kafr el-Dauwar

Lake Mariut

Damanh (Hermopolis Par

Abusir (Taposiris Magna)

◀ A Late Period bronze figure of Wadjit, the goddess of the Delta. She is shown with a lioness's head and an *uraeus* (cobra). The cobra was a symbol of Lower Egypt.

▲ Major city or town
● Other modern town
• Location of ancient site
– – Regional boundary
═ Road
▢ Fertile land

Types of ancient site

▲ Pyramid (with related temples and tombs)
○ Settlement
▼ Temple
■ Tomb
◆ Other

Zifta Modern name
(Buto) Ancient name

Scale 1:1 000 000

0   30 km

0   20 miles

B

C

D

3

Damietta Mouth

Lake Burullus

Damietta

Lake Manzala

el-Balamun
(Diospolis Inferior)

Port Said

Tell el-Farain (Buto)

el-Mataria

Shirbin

Kafr el-Sheikh

Suez Canal

Tell el-Farama
(Pelusium)

Behbeit el-Hagar (Iseum)

el-Mansura

Sa el-Hagar (Sais)

Tell el-Ruba (Mendes)

San el-Hagar (Tanis)

el-Mahalla
el-Kubra

(Naukratis)

el-Baqliya
(Hermopolis Parva)

Tell el-Timai (Thmuis)

Tell Abu Sifa (Sile)

Samannud
(Sebennytos)

Tell Nabasha (Imet)

Kom el-Hisn
(Imu)

el-Simbellawein

Tanta

LOWER EGYPT

Qantir (Pi-Ramesses)

Sweet Water Canal

el-Khatana

Zifta

Mit Ghamr

Abu Kebir

Tell el-Daba
(Avaris)

Tell el-Muqdam
(Leontopolis)

Shibin el-Kom

Saft el-Hinna
(Per-Sopdu)

Tell el-Maskhuta
(Pithom)

Lake Timsah

Zagazig

Tell Basta
(Bubastis)

Ismailia

Suez Canal

Minuf

Wadi Tumilat

Kom Abu Billo
(Terenuthis)

Rosetta Branch

Tell Atrib
(Athribis)

Benha

Ismailia Canal

Damietta Branch

Bilbeis

Great Bitter Lake

Merimda Beni Salama

Little Bitter Lake

Tell el-Yahudiya (Leontopolis)

Sweet Water Canal

Ausim
(Letopolis)

Tell Hisn
(Heliopolis)

Suez Canal

el-Giza

Cairo

Tura

Nile

Suez

MEMPHIS
SEE PAGE 81

Helwan

Zawyet Dahshur

MIDDLE EGYPT
SEE PAGE 75

1

*Birket Qarun
(Lake Moeris)*

Gulf of Suez

Sinnuris

FAIYUM

Medinet el-Faiyum

el-Wasta

el-Lahun

Nile

Ihnasya el-Medina

Beni Suef

2

Town at Bubastis

BUBASTIS WAS AN IMPORTANT TOWN FROM the Old Kingdom onwards. It was the chief cult center of the feline goddess Bastet. The main temple of Bastet was rebuilt many times. Magnificent buildings were put up for Bastet by the 22nd-Dynasty kings, who came from Bubastis.

The annual festival of the goddess was one of the most popular in Egypt. People came from all over the country to sing, dance, and feast in honor of Bastet. One Greek writer commented that "More wine is drunk at this festival than in the whole of the rest of the year" (Herodotus, *History II*).

From the Third Intermediate Period sacred cats were bred in the temple. A special cat cemetery lies to the north of the town. It is not known how many cats were buried there, but it is estimated that there were millions. During the 19th century thousands of cat mummies from Bubastis were shipped to Europe to be ground up and used as fertilizer.

▼ Bronze statuette of a sacred cat from Bubastis. The cat wears a necklace and its ears are pierced for earrings.

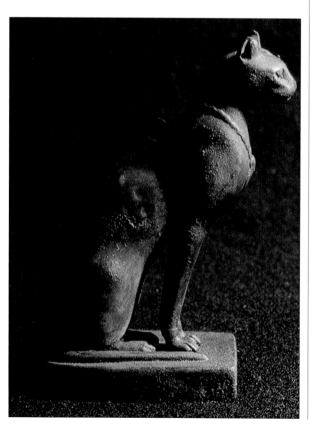

Harbor at Alexandria

ALEXANDRIA, THE CAPITAL OF THE Ptolemies, was a Greek-style city that belonged to the Mediterranean world. A tall lighthouse on an island in the harbor was one of the Seven Wonders of the Ancient World. Other important buildings included the tomb of the city's founder, Alexander the Great, and a library that held the largest collection of books in the ancient world. Under Roman rule a sports stadium, public bath-houses, and villas were built.

Underground tombs survive close to the temple of the Greco-Egyptian god Serapis. These tombs are decorated with scenes from Egyptian religion painted in the Greek style. They show that the Greeks borrowed some Egyptian ideas. In addition, statues and elements from earlier Egyptian buildings were brought to Alexandria to decorate the city. Among them was the pair of obelisks from Heliopolis known as "Cleopatra's Needles."

Some parts of ancient Alexandria are buried deep under the modern city. Others have been lost to the sea as a result of earthquakes and the gradual erosion of the coastline. In the last 15 years French archaeologists have explored the harbor area. Many large statues have been brought up from the seabed where they have been lying for at least 1,700 years.

▼ A diver records the details of a sphinx found on the seabed in Alexandria harbor. This sphinx stood outside a temple or palace until earthquakes and tidal waves destroyed part of the city.

Alexandria • • Tanis
Bubastis • • Qantir
Cairo •

Treasures of Tanis

THE RUINS AT TANIS ARE THE MOST impressive in the whole of the Delta. Tanis was the capital of Egypt for much of the Third Intermediate Period. Inside a double mud-brick enclosure wall lies a great temple of Amon founded by King Psusennes I. This temple was added to by several Third Intermediate Period kings.

Stone blocks, columns, obelisks, and statues of much earlier dates have been found at Tanis. All of them come from older buildings at other sites. They were brought to Tanis to give instant splendor to the new capital.

A golden discovery

In 1939 a French archaeologist named Pierre Montet found underground tombs near the southwest corner of the temple. Four Third Intermediate Period kings had been buried there. Some of the burials were intact. Spectacular gold and silver jewelry as well as gold and silver vessels, including cups, were recovered. King Psusennes I had a solid silver coffin and a golden mummy mask (see page 42).

▼ The ruins of the great temple of Amon at Tanis. The colossal statue of a king was probably moved to Tanis from Pi-Ramesses, the Delta capital built by Ramesses II.

City at Qantir

THE QANTIR AREA WAS TWICE OF GREAT importance in Egyptian history. In the Second Intermediate Period it was the site of Avaris, the capital of the Hyksos kings. Avaris was probably in the south part of the Qantir district, close to modern Tell el-Daba. This Hyksos city was taken and partly destroyed by the Theban king Ahmose in about 1540 B.C.E.

The Ramessid family came from this area of the Delta. Ramesses II built a new city called Pi-Ramesses close to modern Qantir. It was one of the largest and most splendid cities in Egypt. The palace area alone covered nearly 22 acres (9 ha)—which is the equivalent of nine soccer fields.

Almost nothing is left, however. Many of the main buildings were later dismantled to provide stone and statues for Tanis. It was probably forced labor on the building of Pi-Ramesses that led to the Exodus of the Jews from Egypt.

▼ This bronze bust of a king probably comes from the Qantir area and may have been part of a larger statue.

Glossary

Book of the Dead Spells written on papyrus and placed in tombs from the New Kingdom to the Greco-Roman Period. No single copy contains all 192 spells.

canopic jars Set of four jars to hold the vital organs removed from a mummy. The organs were the liver, lungs, stomach, and intestines.

cartouche A sign representing an oval knot of rope. From the Fourth Dynasty, the king's two most important names were written inside cartouches. Cartouches were used on the king's documents and made into reliefs on the king's buildings and statues as a kind of seal.

Cataracts Stretches of dangerous rapids in the Nile River. There were six Cataracts between Aswan and Khartoum in Sudan.

colonnade A double row of columns roofed to form a passage, or a single row of columns joined by a roof to a wall.

cuneiform The Mesopotamian script, written on clay tablets with wedge-shaped strokes. Tablets with cuneiform texts were found at el-Amarna.

deity A god or goddess. Many Egyptian deities can have human, semihuman, and animal shapes.

demotic An Egyptian script for everyday use, developed in the seventh century B.C.E. It is one of the three scripts on the Rosetta Stone.

dynasty A series of rulers, usually related to each other by blood or marriage. The order of the dynasties is known from the third-century B.C.E. historian Manetho and from ancient Egyptian lists of kings.

faience Egyptian faience (glazed pottery) was made by baking quartz sand with other mineral ingredients. The most common colors are green and blue.

figurine A small statue of a god or goddess, a person or an animal. Figurines could be made of stone, wood, metal, faience, or pottery.

findspot Place where an ancient body or object was found by archaeologists.

hieratic An Egyptian script used on papyrus and ostraca. It was developed from the hieroglyphic script.

hieroglyph A sign in the oldest Egyptian script. Most hieroglyphic signs are pictures of people, animals, plants, or things. The word is Greek and means "sacred carving."

inundation The annual flooding of the Nile River between July and October. A "good Nile" was a flood that covered all the agricultural land, leaving behind a fertile layer of mud. If the flood was too high, it swept away houses. If the flood was too low, it would not cover all the fields. These were "bad Niles."

ka The spirit or "double" of a living person. After death the *ka* needed offerings to survive. A dead person also had a *ba* (soul), shown as a human-headed bird.

mastaba A type of Early Dynastic and Old Kingdom tomb with a flat-roofed rectangular superstructure. The name comes from the Arabic word for a bench.

mummification The artificial preservation of bodies. Drying out the body was usually the most important part of the process.

natron A natural mixture of carbonate, bicarbonate, chloride, and sodium sulfate. It was used in mummification and was an ingredient of faience.

necropolis A Greek term meaning "city of the dead." It is used for large and important burial areas. These were mainly on the edge of the desert.

nome Greek word for an administrative province of Egypt. The governor of a nome was a nomarch.

obelisk A tapering stone shaft with a tip shaped like a pyramid. A symbol of the sun's rays. Pairs of obelisks were often set up outside temples.

oracle A shrine where a god or goddess answered questions from worshipers, or a sign that was given by a deity in answer to a question.

ostracon A flake of limestone or a broken piece of pottery used for writing or drawing on. Most texts on ostraca are in hieratic or demotic.

papyrus A marsh plant (*Cyperus papyrus*) and a type of paper made from it. Also a scroll made from sheets of papyrus gummed together.

pharaoh A title for the king of Egypt from the late 18th Dynasty onward. It means "The Great House"—the Palace.

pylon The grand entrance to a temple, consisting of towers flanking a doorway.

pyramid A tomb in the shape of a geometric pyramid. This shape may have symbolized a stairway to heaven, the sun's rays, or the first mound of land.

relief A scene carved in stone or wood.

sacred bark A special boat used by a statue of a deity on river journeys. Statues were often carried in model boats known as bark shrines.

sarcophagus Used in this book to mean the stone chest that a coffin was placed inside. A sarcophagus was rectangular or anthropoid (human body-shaped).

scarab A carving in the form of a scarab beetle (dung beetle). It represented Khepri, god of the rising sun. This "sun beetle" was a very popular amulet shape. Scarabs were often inscribed with royal names.

scribe A person trained to read and write. Most scribes worked for the government.

shabti (or *ushabti*) Small figurines, usually in the shape of a mummy, placed in burials. Their magical purpose was to carry out any work the dead person might be told to do in the afterlife.

sphinx An Egyptian sphinx usually had the body of a lion and the head of a king or queen. It was a symbol of royal power and a form of the sun god.

stela A slab of stone or wood, usually with carved and painted texts and scenes. Stelae were set up in the outer areas of tombs and in temples somewhat like gravestones or commemorative plaques.

uraeus A symbol of kingship in the shape of a rearing cobra.

vizier The highest official in the Egyptian government. There were sometimes two viziers, one based at Memphis, the other at Thebes.

FURTHER READING

Books for young people
Ardagh, P. *The Hieroglyphs Handbook* (Scholastic, 2001).
Clare, J. D. *Pyramids of Ancient Egypt* (Harcourt Brace Jovanich, 1992).
Cohen, D. *Ancient Egypt* (Doubleday, 1990).
Galford, E. *Hatshepsut: The Princess Who Became King* (National Geographic, 2005).
Harris, G. *Gods and Pharaohs from Egyptian Mythology* (Shocken, 1983).
Harris, G., and D. Pemberton. *The British Museum Illustrated Encyclopaedia of Ancient Egypt* (NTC, 2000).
Hawass, Z. *Tutankhamun: The Mystery of the Boy King* (National Geographic, 2005).
Ikram, S. *Egyptology* (Amideast, 1997).
Millard, A. *Going to War in Ancient Egypt* (Franklin Watts, 2001).
Pemberton, D. *Egyptian Mummies: People from the Past* (Harcourt, 2000).
Tiano, O. *Rameses II and Egypt* (Henry Holt & Co., 1996).

Reference books for adults
Baines, J., and J. Malek. *Cultural Atlas of Ancient Egypt* (Checkmark Books, 2000).
Ikram, S., and A. Dodson. *The Mummy in Ancient Egypt* (W. W. Norton & Co., 1998).
Lehner, M. *The Complete Pyramids* (W. W. Norton & Co., 1997).
Pinch, G. *Handbook of Egyptian Mythology* (ABC-Clio, 2002).
Redford, D. (ed.). *The Oxford Encyclopaedia of Ancient Egypt* (Oxford University Press, 2001).
Taylor, J. H. *Death and the Afterlife in Ancient Egypt* (University of Chicago Press, 2001).

Egyptology and museum Web sites with sections for young people
http://www.ancientegypt.co.uk
Pages about Egypt on the Web site of the British Museum, London.

www.ashmol.ox.ac.uk/Griffith.html
The Griffith Institute of Oxford, England, includes links for young people.

http://www.carlos.emory.edu/ODYSSEY
An interactive journey through ancient Egypt.

http://www.oi.uchicago.edu/OI/MUS/ED
The Oriental Institute of the University of Chicago education program.

http://www.guardians.net/egypt/kids
Fun and interesting Egypt links especially for children.

http://www.historyforkids.org
Community service learning project from Portland State University. Click on link to Egypt.

http://www.horus.ics.org.eg
Egyptian Web site designed and developed specially for kids around the world.

http://www.metmuseum.org/explore
The Metropolitan Museum of Art "Explore and Learn" pages with links to ancient Egyptian art.

Gazetteer

The gazetteer lists places and features, such as islands or rivers, found on the maps. Each has a separate entry including a page and grid reference number. For example:
Abydos 59 B2

Sometimes a modern place also has an ancient name form. This name is added to the entry before the page number. For example:
Aniba (Miam) 55 A2

All features are shown in italic type. For example:
Atbara, r. 11 D3

A letter after the feature describes the kind of feature:
d. district: *i.* island; *o.* oasis;
r. river

Abahuda 55 A2
Abnub 75 B1
Abu Kebir 89 C2
Abu Simbel 55 A2
Abydos 59 B2
Addis Ababa 11 D2
Aden 11 E2
Akhmim (Panopolis) 71 B2
Aksha 54 A2
Albert, Lake 11 C1
Albert Nile, r. 11 C1
Alexandria (Alexandria) 11 C4, 88 A3
Allaqi, Wadi 55 C2
Amada 55 B2
Amman 11 D4
Aniba (Miam) 55 A2
Armant (Hermonthis) 59 B3
Aswan (Elephantine) 11 D4, 55 B4, 59 B2
Aswan Dam 59 B2
Aswan High Dam 55 B3, 59 B1
Asyut 11 C4, 75 B1
Asyut (Lykopolis) 71 B3, 75 B1
Atbara, r. 11 D3
Atfih (Aphroditopolis) 75 B3
Ausim (Letopolis) 89 C2

Baghdad 11 E5
Bahr Yusuf, r. 75 A2
Bahariya, o. 11 C4
Behbeit el-Hagar 89 C3
Beirut 11 D5
Beit el-Wali 55 B3
Benha 89 C2
Beni Hasan 75 A1

Beni Mazar 75 A2
Beni Suef 89 C1, 75 B3
Biga 59 B2
Bilbeis 89 C2
Birket Qarun (Lake Moeris) 75 A3, 89 B1
Blue Nile, r. 11 D2
Buhen 54 A1
Burullus, Lake 89 B3

Cairo 11 C4, 89 C2
Catherine, Mount 11 D4
Chad 10 B3
Crete, i. 11 C5

Dabod 55 B3
Dahshur 89 C1
Dairut 70 A3, 75 A1
Dakhla, o. 11 C4
Damanhur (Hermopolis Parva) 88 B3
Damascus 11 D5
Damietta 89 C3
Damietta Branch, r. 89 C2
Deir el-Gabrawi 75 B1
Deir el-Bersha 75 A1
Democratic Republic of Congo 11 C1
Dendara (Iunet) 71 C2
Dendur (Tutzis) 55 B3
Dibeira East 54 A2
Dibeira West 54 A2
Dunqul, o. 11 C3

Eastern Desert 11 C4, 59 C4, 71 C2
Edfu (Apollinopolis Magna) 59 B2
Egypt 11 C4, 55 A2
el-Amarna (Akhetaten) 71 A3, 75 A1
el-Ashmunein (Hermopolis) 75 A1
el-Badari 71 B2
el-Bahnasa (Oxyrhynchus) 75 A2
el-Baqliya (Hermopolis Parva) 89 C2
el-Derr 55 B2
el-Fashn 75 A2
el-Hella (Contra-Lato) 59 B3
el-Hiba (Ankyronon Polis) 75 A2
el-Kab (Nekheb) 59 B3
el-Kharga, o. 11 C4
el-Khatana 89 C2
el-Kula 59 B3
el-Lahun 75 B3
el-Lessiya 55 B2
el-Lisht (Itjtawy) 75 B3, 89 C1
el-Mahalla el Kubra 89 C2
el-Mansura 89 C3
el-Maragha 71 B2
el-Matariya 89 D3
el-Minya (Menat-Khufu) 75

A2
el-Moalla 59 B3
el-Qasr wa'l Saiyad (Khenoboskion) 71 C2
el-Qusiya (Cusae) 75 A1
el-Rizeiqat 59 B3
el-Sheikh Said 75 A1
el-Simbellawein 89 C2
el-Wasta 75 B3, 89 C1
Eritrea 11 E2
Esna (Latopolis) 59 B3, 71 C1
Ethiopia 11 D2
Euphrates, r. 11 E5

Faiyum, d. 11 C4, 75 A3, 89 B1
Farafra, o. 11 C4
Faras 54 A2

Gebel el-Silsila 59 B2
Gebelein (Per-Hathor) 59 B3, 71 C1
Gerf Hussein 55 B3
Girga (Thinis) 71 B2
Great Bitter Lake 89 D2

Hawara 75 A3
Helwan 89 C1
Hiw (Diospolis Parva) 59 B3, 71 C1

Idku, Lake 88 B3
Ihnasya el-Medina (Herakleopolis) 75 A3
Iraq 11 E5
Ismailia 89 D2
Ismailia Canal 89 C2
Israel 11 D5

Jerusalem 11 D4
Jordan 11 D4

Kafr el-Sheikh 89 B3
Khartoum 11 D2
Kom Abu Billo (Terenuthis) 89 B2
Kom el-Ahmar (Hierakonpolis) 59 B3
Kom el-Hisn 89 B2
Kom Medinet Ghurab 75 A3
Kom Mer 59 B3
Kom Ombo (Ombos) 59 B2
Kor 54 A1
Kurkur, o. 11 D3
Kuwait 11 E4

Lebanon 11 D5
Libya 10 B4
Libyan Desert 11 B4
Little Bitter Lake 89 D2
Lower Egypt, d. 89 B2
Lower Nubia, d. 55 A2
Luxor (Thebes) 59 B3, 71 C1

Maidum 75 B3
Mallawi 70 A3, 75 A1
Manfalut 71 A3, 75 A1
Manzala, Lake 89 C3
Mariut, Lake 88 A3
Medinet el-Faiyum (Krokodilopolis) 75 A3, 89 B1
Meir (Cusae) 75 A1
Memphis 89 C1
Merimda Ben Salama 89 B2
Middle Egypt, d. 71 B3, 75 A2, 89 B1
Minuf 89 B2
Mirgissa (Iqen) 54 A1
Mit Ghamr 89 C2
Mogadishu 11 E1

Nafud, o. 11 E4
Nag el-Madamud 71 C1
Naqada (Ombos/Nubt) 71 C1
Nasser, Lake 11 D3, 55 B3, 59 B1
Naukratis 89 B2
New el-Sebua 55 B2
New Kalabsha 55 B3
Nile, r. 11 D3, 59 B3, 71 B2, 75 B3
Northern Upper Egypt, d. 59 B4, 71 B2, 75 B1
Nubia, d. 55 B3, 59 B1
Nubian Desert 11 D3

Old el-Sebua 55 B2
Old Kalabsha (Talmis) 55 B3

Philae 55 B4, 59 B2
Port Said 89 D3

Qantir 89 C2
Qasr Ibrim (Primis) 55 B2
Qasr el-Sagha 75 A3
Qattara Depression 11 C4
Qaw el-Kebir (Antaeopolis) 71 B2
Qena (Kaine) 59 B4, 71 C2
Qift (Koptos) 59 B3, 71 C1
Qus (Apollinopolis Parva) 71 C1
Qustul 55 A2

Riyadh 11 E4
Rosetta 88 B3
Rosetta Branch, r. 89 B2

Sa el-Hagar (Sais) 89 B2
Saft el-Hinna (Per-Sopdu) 89 C2
Sahara Desert 10 A4
Samalut 75 A2
San'a 11 E2
San el-Hagar (Tanis) 89 C2
Saudi Arabia 11 E4
Seila 75 B3
Serra East 54 A2

Shibin el-Kom 89 B2
Shirbin 89 C3
Sidmant el-Gebel 75 A3
Sinai, Mount 11 D4
Siwa, o. 11 C4
Sohag 71 B2
Somalia 11 E2
Southern Upper Egypt, d. 55 B4, 59 B3, 71 C1
Speos Artemidos 75 A1
Sudan 11 C2, 55 A1
Suez 89 D1
Suez Canal 11 D4, 89 D3
Syria 11 D5

Tafa (Taphis) 55 B3
Tahta 71 B2
Tanta 89 B2
Tell Abu Sefa (Sile) 89 D2
Tell Atrib (Athribis) 89 C2
Tell Basta (Bubastis) 89 C2
Tell el-Daba (Avaris/pi-Ramesses) 89 C2
Tell el-Farain (Buto) 89 B3
Tell el-Farama (Pelusium) 89 D3
Tell el-Maskuta (Pithom) 89 D2
Tell el-Muqdam (Leontopolis) 89 C2
Tell el-Timai (Thumis) 89 C2
Tell el-Ruba (Mendes) 89 C2
Tell el-Yahudiya (Leontopolis) 89 C2
Tell Hisn (Heliopolis) 89 C2
Tell Nabasha 89 C2
Tigris, r. 11 E5
Tihna (Akoris) 75 A2
Tima 71 B2
Timsah, Lake 89 D2
Tod 59 B3, 71 C1
Tripoli 10 A5
Tumilat, Wadi 89 C2
Tuna el-Gebel (Hermopolis) 75 A1
Tura 89 C1

Umm el-Qaab 71 B2
Upper Nubia, d. 55 A1

Valley of the Kings 59 B3, 71 C1

Wadi Halfa 11 C3, 54 A1
Wannina (Athribis) 71 B2
Western Desert 11 C4, 59 A3, 71 B1, 75 A2
White Nile, r. 11 D2

Yemen 11 E2

Zagazig 89 C2
Zawyet el-Amwat 75 A2
Zifta 89 C2

Index